I0118810

James Parker

A Retail Catalogue of Books

James Parker

A Retail Catalogue of Books

ISBN/EAN: 9783742806826

Manufactured in Europe, USA, Canada, Australia, Japa

Cover: Foto ©Thomas Meinert / pixelio.de

Manufactured and distributed by brebook publishing software
(www.brebook.com)

James Parker

A Retail Catalogue of Books

A RETAIL

CATALOGUE OF BOOKS, &c.

PUBLISHED BY

MESSRS. JAMES PARKER & CO.

OXFORD,

AND 377, STRAND, LONDON.

1874.

SUMMARY OF CONTENTS.

THEOLOGICAL WORKS.—On the Creeds; on Eucharistical Adoration; on Confession, p. 3. On Christian Evidences; Theology; the Future State, p. 4. Thirty-nine Articles, Anglican Orders, p. 5. Church of England and Rome, p. 6. Ancient Doctrinal Treatises, p. 7.

THE HOLY SCRIPTURES, p. 8. The Psalms, Prophets, S. Paul's Epistles, p. 9. The Four Gospels and Acts, p. 10.

THE PRAYER-BOOK.—The Lord's Prayer, Epistles and Gospels, Ordination Service, p. 11.

ECCLESIASTICAL HISTORY, pp. 12, 13.

LIBRARY OF THE FATHERS.—Translations, p. 14; Original Texts, p. 15.

ANGLO-CATHOLIC LIBRARY.—Re-issue, pp. 16, 17; Works, pp. 18, 19.

SERMONS, pp. 20, 21, 22. By Dr. Pusey, pp. 23, 24.

BIOGRAPHIES, p. 25.

SACRED POETRY.—The Christian Year, &c., p. 26; Isaac Williams' Poetical Works, p. 27; Sacred Poetry, &c., pp. 28, 29.

DEVOTIONAL WORKS, p. 30; Edited by Dr. Pusey, p. 31; Private and Family Prayers, p. 32; for Various Occasions, &c., p. 33; for the Lord's Supper, p. 34; the Practical Christian's Library, p. 34; Oxford Series of Devotional Works, p. 35; the Christian Seasons, p. 36; the Daily Service-book, p. 37.

CHURCH PSALMODY.—Psalters, Anthems, and Hymn-books, p. 38.

PAROCHIAL.—Parish Work; Pastoral Visitation; Miscellanea, p. 39, Catechism; Baptism, p. 40. Confirmation; The Lord's Supper; Prayer-book; Public Worship, p. 41. Historical Tales, p. 42. Tales and Allegories, &c., p. 43. Tales for Young Men; Tales from the "Penny Post;" Fairy Tales, &c., p. 44. Cottage Pictures and Scripture Prints; The "Penny Post," p. 45. Tracts for Parochial Use, pp. 46, 47, 48.

ARCHITECTURAL WORKS, p. 49. Archæological Works, pp. 50, 51. Topographical Works, pp. 52, 53. Practical Architecture, p. 54.

EDUCATIONAL.—The Oxford Pocket Classics, p. 55. Texts with Short Notes, pp. 56, 57. Octavo Editions of Classics; Translations, &c., p. 58. Educational Works—Greek, Latin, French, and Hebrew, p. 59; Mathematical, Logic, &c., p. 60. Examination Papers; University of Oxford, p. 61. Scientific, p. 62. Historical, p. 63. Miscellaneous, p. 64.

Theological Works.

On the Creeds.

A SHORT EXPLANATION OF THE NICENE CREED, for the Use of Persons beginning the Study of Theology. By A. P. Forbes, D.C.L., Bishop of Brechin. Second Edition, Crown 8vo., cloth, 6s.

A DEFENCE OF THE NICENE CREED out of the extant writings of the Catholic Doctors who flourished during the three first centuries of the Christian Church. By George Bull, D.D., Lord Bishop of St. David's. A new Translation. 2 vols., 8vo., 10s.

A CRITICAL HISTORY OF THE ATHANASIAN CREED, by the Rev. Daniel Waterland, D.D. Fcap. 8vo., cloth, 5s.

On Eucharistical Adoration.

ON EUCHARISTICAL ADORATION. By the late Rev. John Keble, M.A., Vicar of Hursley.—With Considerations suggested by a late Pastoral Letter (1858) on the Doctrine of the Most Holy Eucharist. 8vo., cloth, 6s. A Cheap Edition, 24mo., sewed, 2s.

THE DOCTRINE OF THE REAL PRESENCE, as contained in the Fathers from the death of St. John the Evangelist to the 4th General Council. 1855. 12s.

THE REAL PRESENCE, the Doctrine of the English Church, with a Vindication of the Reception by the wicked and of the Adoration of our Lord Jesus Christ truly present. 8vo., 7s. 6d.

THE HISTORY OF POPISH TRANSUBSTANTIATION. By John Cosin, D.D., Lord Bishop of Durham. A new Edition, revised. Fcap. 8vo., cloth, 2s. 6d.

THE TEACHING OF THE ANGLICAN DIVINES of the time of King James I. and King Charles I. on the Doctrine of the Holy Eucharist, extracted from their Writings. By H. C. Groves, A.M., Curate of Kilmore. 8vo., sewed, 3s. 6d.

The Power of the Priesthood in Absolution,

THE POWER OF THE PRIESTHOOD IN ABSOLUTION, and a Few Remarks on Confession; with an Appendix, containing a List of Documents, and of Eminent Christians who have used Absolution; and Quotations from Eminent English Divines. By William Cooke, M.A., F.S.A., Hon. Canon of Chester. Second Edition, 18mo., sewed, 2s.

THE CHURCH OF ENGLAND LEAVES HER CHILDREN FREE TO WHOM TO OPEN THEIR GRIEFS. A Letter to the Rev. W. U. Richards. 8vo., with Postscript, 5s.

The Doctrine of Justification.

JUSTIFICATION: being the Bampton Lectures for 1845. By Charles A. Heurtley, B.D., Canon of Ch. Ch., Oxford. 8vo., cloth, 9s.

THEOLOGICAL WORKS (continued).

Christian Evidences, &c.

CHARACTERISTICS OF CHRISTIAN MORALITY. The Hampton Lectures for the year 1878. By the Rev. I. GREGORY SMITH, M.A., late Fellow of Brasenose College ; Vicar of Malvern ; and Prebendary of Hereford. 8vo., cloth, 6s.

APOLLOS ; or, THE WAY OF GOD. A Plea for the Religion of Scripture. By A. CLEVELAND COXE, Bishop of Western New York. Crown 8vo.   [Just ready.

THE NATURE AND COMPARATIVE VALUE OF THE CHRISTIAN EVIDENCES CONSIDERED GENERALLY. Being the Hampton Lectures for 1849. By R. MICHELL, B.D., Principal of Magdalen Hall. 8vo., cloth, 10s. 6d.

ON MEANS OF ATTAINING CHRISTIAN TRUTH. An Inquiry into the connected uses of the Principal Means of Attaining Christian Truth, being the Hampton Lectures for 1840. By EDWARD HAWKINS, D.D., Provost of Oriel, and Canon of Rochester. Second Edition. 8vo., cloth, 10s. 6d.

A SYSTEMATIC ANALYSIS OF BISHOP BUTLER'S COM-PLETE TREATISE ON THE ANALOGY OF NATURAL AND RE-VEALED RELIGION TO THE CONSTITUTION AND COURSE OF NATURE, on the Plan of the Rev. Dr. MILL'S Analysis of Bishop PEARSON's Exposition of the Creed. By JOHN WILKINSON, M.A., of Merton College, Oxford, and Prebendary of Sarum. 8vo., cloth, 2s. 6d.

CHRISTIAN FAITH COMPREHENSIVE, NOT PARTIAL; DEFINITE, NOT UNCERTAIN. Being the Hampton Lectures for 1857. By WILLIAM EDWARD JELF, D.D., 8vo., cloth, 7s. 6d.

CHRISTIAN POLITICS. By the Rev. WILLIAM SEWELL, D.D., Fellow and Sub-Rector of Exeter College, Oxford. Fcap. 8vo., cloth, 6s.

PLEAS FOR THE FAITH. Especially Designed for the Use of Missionaries at Home and Abroad, by the Rev. W. SOMERVILLE LACH-SZYRMA, M.A., St. Augustine's College, Canterbury. Fcap. 8vo., limp cloth, 2s. 6d.

The Study of Theology.

LECTURES ON THE STUDY OF THEOLOGY, delivered in the Chapel of Oriel College, Oxford, by the Rev. CHARLES P. CHRETIEN, M.A., Fellow and Tutor of Oriel. 8vo., cloth, 5s.

The Future State.

ON THE EXISTENCE OF THE SOUL AFTER DEATH : a Dissertation opposed to the Principles of Priestley, Law, and their respective Followers. By R. LAURENCE, Archbishop of Cashel. 8vo., 8s. 6d.

CONSIDERATIONS RESPECTING A FUTURE STATE : AN ESSAY. By the Rev. Lewis P. MERCIER, M.A., University College, Oxford. Crown 8vo., cloth, 4s.

THEOLOGICAL WORKS (*continued*).

The XXXIX. Articles.

AN EXPLANATION OF THE THIRTY-NINE ARTICLES. With an Epistle Dedicatory to the Rev. E. B. Pusey, D.D. By A. P. Forbes, D.C.L., Bishop of Brechin. Second Edition, in one vol., Post 8vo., 12s.

ARTICULI ECCLESIÆ ANGLICANÆ; or, The Several Editions of the Articles of the Church of England, as set forth *temp.* King Edward VI. and Queen Elizabeth, arranged in one Comparative View. By William H. Davey, M.A., late Vice-Principal of Cuddesdon Theological College. 8vo., cloth, 2s. 6d.

LECTURES ON THE ARTICLES OF THE UNITED CHURCH OF ENGLAND AND IRELAND. By J. D. Macbride, D.C.L. 8vo., cloth, 12s.

AN ATTEMPT TO ILLUSTRATE THOSE ARTICLES OF THE CHURCH OF ENGLAND which the Calvinists improperly considered as Calvinistical. Being the Hampton Lectures for 1804. By Richard Laurence, LL.D., Abp. of Cashel. 8vo., cloth, 3s. 6d.

TRACT XC. On certain Passages in the XXXIX. Articles, by the Rev. J. H. Newman, M.A., 1841; with Historical Preface by E. B. Pusey, D.D.; and Catholic Subscription to the XXXIX. Articles considered in reference to Tract XC., by the Rev. John Keble, M.A., 1861. 8vo., sewed, 1s. 6d.

DOCUMENTARY ILLUSTRATIONS of the PRINCIPLES to be KEPT IN VIEW in the INTERPRETATION OF THE THIRTY-NINE ARTICLES. By William B. Heathcote, B.C.L. 8vo., sewed, 6s.

Anglican Orders.

ORDINUM SACRORUM IN ECCLESIA ANGLICANA DEFENSIO unacum Statutis, Documentis, et Testimoniis ordinum Anglicorum valorem probantibus; et Registro Consecrationis Archiepiscopi Parkeri, in Bibliotheca Lambethæ Asservato. Photolincographice expresso. Editore T. J. Bailey, B.A., e Coll. C. C. Cantab. Ecclesiæ Anglicanæ Sacerdote. Large Folio, cloth, £1 10s.

A DEFENCE OF HOLY ORDERS IN THE CHURCH OF ENGLAND, including the Statutes, Documents, and other Evidence attesting the Validity of Anglican Orders. Edited by the Rev. T. J. Bailey, B.A., C.C. Coll., Cambridge. Crown 8vo., cloth, 6s.

THE JURISDICTION AND MISSION OF THE ANGLICAN EPISCOPATE. By the Rev. T. J. Bailey. Crown 8vo., limp cloth, 2s.

ENGLISH ORDERS AND PAPAL SUPREMACY: A Brief Manual of Historical Facts. By the Rev. T. J. Bailey. Crown 8vo., limp cloth, 1s. 6d.

A DISSERTATION ON THE VALIDITY OF THE ORDINATIONS of the English, and of the Succession of the Bishops of the Anglican Church; with Proofs, &c. By Father le Courayer. 8vo., cloth, 6s.

THE ADMINISTRATION OF THE HOLY SPIRIT IN THE BODY OF CHRIST. Eight Lectures preached before the University of Oxford in the Year 1868, on the Foundation of the late Rev. John Bampton, M.A., Canon of Salisbury. By the Right Rev. the Lord Bishop of Salisbury. Second Edition, Crown 8vo., 7s. 6d.

6   *JAMES PARKER AND CO.*

THEOLOGICAL WORKS (*continued*).

The Church of England.

AN INQUIRY INTO THE MEANS OF GRACE, their Mutual Connection, and combined Use, with especial reference to the Church of England. Being the Bampton Lectures for 1844. By RICHARD WILLIAM JELF, D.D., Canon of Christ Church, Oxford. 8vo., cloth, 10s. 6d.

THE AUTHORITATIVE TEACHING OF THE CHURCH shewn to be in Conformity with Scripture Analogy, and the Moral Constitution of Man. Being the Bampton Lectures for 1839. By H. A. WOODGATE, B.D., Fellow of St. John's College, Oxford. 8vo. cloth, 10s.

THE ABSENCE OF PRECISION in the Formularies of the Church of England, Scriptural, and suitable to a State of Probation. Being the Bampton Lectures for 1858, by JOHN ERNEST BODE, M.A., Rector of Westwell. 8vo., cloth, 8s.

AN APOLOGY OF THE CHURCH OF ENGLAND; and an Epistle to Seignior Scipio concerning the Council of Trent. By JOHN JEWELL, D.D., Lord Bishop of Salisbury. Fcap. 8vo. cloth, 3s. 6d.

LETTER TO THE LORD BISHOP OF LONDON, in Explanation of some Statements contained in a Letter by the Rev. W. DODSWORTH. By the Rev. E. B. PUSEY, D.D. Fifth Thousand. 16mo., 1s.

THE ROYAL SUPREMACY not an Arbitrary Authority, but limited by the Laws of the Church of which Kings are Members. Ancient Precedents. By the Rev. E. B. PUSEY, D.D. 8vo., 7s.

JONES' (of Nayland) TRACTS ON THE CHURCH. Cloth, 1s. 6d.

JONES' ESSAY ON THE CHURCH. Fcap. 8vo., 1s.

HAMMOND'S PARENESIS. A Discourse of Heresy in Defence of our Church against the Romanist. 18mo., cloth, 1s. 6d.

A PLAIN ARGUMENT for the CHURCH, on a Card. 1d.

TEN REASONS WHY I LOVE MY CHURCH. 18 for 3d.

PLAIN TESTIMONIES IN FAVOUR OF EPISCOPACY. 4 pp., 8vo., ½d.

WORDSWORTH'S CREDENDA: A Summary of the Apostles' Creed, &c., 4d.

KEBLE'S SELECTIONS FROM HOOKER. 18mo., 1s. 6d.

VINCENT OF LIRINS AGAINST HERESY. 18mo., 1s. 6d.

PYE'S TWO LECTURES ON THE HOLY CATHOLIC CHURCH. 18mo., 1s. 6d.

MANT'S (Bishop) DUTY AND ADVANTAGE OF CHURCH COMMUNION. 4d.

PASCAL'S (BLAISE) THOUGHTS ON RELIGION. 18mo., cloth, 1s. 6d.

DOCTRINE OF THE CATHOLIC CHURCH. 8vo., 2s.

CHURCH AND WESLEYANS. 18mo., 3d.

The Church of Rome.

AN EIRENICON. Vol. I. Letter to the Author of the "Christian Year," "The Church of England a Portion of Christ's One Holy Catholic Church, and a Means of Restoring Visible Unity." By the Rev. E. B. PUSEY, D.D. Seventh Thousand. 8vo., cloth, 7s. 6d.

———— Vol. II. First Letter to Dr. NEWMAN, "The Reverential Love due to the ever-blessed Theotokos, and the Doctrine of her 'Immaculate Conception.'" 8vo., cloth, 7s. 6d.

———— Vol. III. Second Letter to Dr. NEWMAN, "Is Healthful Re-union Impossible?" 8vo., cloth, 6s.

TRACTATUS DE VERITATE Conceptionis Beatissimæ Virginis, pro Facienda Relatione coram Patribus Concilii Basilææ, A.D. 1437. Compilatus per Rev. P. FRATREM JOANNEM DE TURRECREMATA, S.T.P., Ordinis Prædicatorum, Tunc Sacri Apostolici Palatii Magistrum. Small 4to., cl., 12s.

PERDITA AND ANGELINA; or, Romeward and Homeward: an Anglo-Roman Dialogue. By C. E. KENNAWAY, M.A., Vicar of Campden. 12mo., cloth, 3s. 6d.

OXFORD, AND 377, STRAND, LONDON.

THEOLOGICAL WORKS (continued).

Ancient Doctrinal Treatises, &c.

THE PASTORAL RULE OF ST. GREGORY. Sancti Gregorii Papæ Regulæ Pastoralis Liber, ad Johannem Episcopum Civitatis Ravennæ. With an English Translation. By the Rev. H. R. Bramley, M.A., Fellow of Magdalen College, Oxford. Fcap. 8vo., cloth, price 6s.

DE FIDE ET SYMBOLO: Documenta quædam nec non Aliquorum SS. Patrum Tractatus. Edidit Carolus A. Heurtley, S.T.P., Dom. Margaretæ Prælector, et Ædis Christi Canonicus. Fcap. 8vo., cloth, 4s. 6d.

S. AURELIUS AUGUSTINUS, Episcorus Hipponensis, De Catechizandis Rudibus, de Fide Rerum quæ non videntur, de Utilitate Credendi. In Usum Juniorum. Edidit C. Marriott, S.T.B., olim Coll. Oriel. Socius. A New Edition, Fcap. 8vo., cloth, 3s. 6d.

ANALECTA CHRISTIANA, In usum Tironum. Edidit et Annotationibus illustravit C. Marriott, S.T.B. 8vo., 10s. 6d.

ST. CYRIL, Archbishop of Alexandria. The Three Epistles (ad Nestorium, ii., iii., et ad Joan Antioch). A Revised Text, with an old Latin Version and an English Translation. Edited by P. E. Pusey, M.A. 8vo., in wrapper, 3s.

CUR DEUS HOMO, or Why God was made Man; by St. Anselm, sometime Archbishop of Canterbury. Translated into English, with an Introduction, &c. Second Edition, Fcap. 8vo., 2s. 6d.

THE BOOK OF RATRAMN the Priest and Monk of Corbey, commonly called Bertram, on the Body and Blood of the Lord. (Latin and English.) To which is added AN APPENDIX, containing the Saxon Homily of Ælfric. Fcap. 8vo. [Nearly ready.

A TRACT ON HOLY VIRGINITY, derived from S. Ambrose, by A. J. Christie, M.A., Fellow of Oriel College, Oxford, 12mo., 2s.

ST. ALDHELM. Sancti Aldhelmi ex Abbate Malmesburiensi Episcopi Schireburnensis Opera quæ extant omnia e Codicibus MSS. emendavit; nonnulla nunc Primum Edidit J. A. Giles, LL.D., C.C.C., Oxon. 8vo., cloth, 5s.

THE CANONS. The Definitions of the Catholic Faith and Canons of Discipline of the First Four General Councils of the Universal Church. In Greek and English. Fcap. 8vo., cloth, 2s. 6d.

CANONES SS. APOSTOLORUM GRÆCE. Cum Versione Anglica et Notis Johnsoni. 8vo., sewed, 2s.

See also the Library of the Fathers, p. 14, and the Bibliotheca Patrum, p. 15.

The Holy Scriptures.

INSPIRATION AND INTERPRETATION. Seven Sermons preached before the University of Oxford; with an Introduction, being an answer to "Essays and Reviews." By the Rev. JOHN W. BURGON, M.A., Fellow of Oriel College; Select Preacher. 8vo., cloth, 14s.

DISCOURSES ON PROPHECY. In which are considered its Structure, Use and Inspiration. By JOHN DAVISON, B.D. Sixth and Cheaper Edition. 8vo., cloth, 9s.

A SHORT SUMMARY OF THE EVIDENCES FOR THE BIBLE. By the Rev. T. S. ACKLAND, M.A., Incumbent of Pollington-cum-Balne, Yorkshire. 18mo., cloth, 8s.

CHRISTIAN VESTIGES OF CREATION. By WILLIAM SEWELL, D.D. 8vo., cloth, 4s. 6d.

AN INTRODUCTORY SKETCH OF SACRED HISTORY; being a Concise Digest of Notes and Extracts from the Bible, and from the Works of approved Authors. 8vo., cloth, 7s. 6d.

SYNCHRONISTICAL ANNALS OF THE KINGS AND PRO-PHETS OF ISRAEL AND JUDAH, and of the Kings of Syria, Assyria, Babylon, and Egypt, mentioned in the Scriptures. 4to., sewed, 7s. 6d.

ON THE PRINCIPLES adopted by Writers who have recommended a New Translation of the Bible. By ARCHBISHOP LAURENCE. 8vo., 5s.

THE STUDENT'S MANUAL OF SCRIPTURE NAMES, IN ALPHABETICAL ORDER; with Scripture References, and Short Historical Notices. For the Use of Schools, Families, and Students preparing for Public Examinations. Fcap. 8vo., limp cloth, 3s.

AN ESSAY ON THE CHRONOLOGY OF THE NEW TESTA-MENT. By THOMAS LEWIN, Trinity College, Oxford. 8vo., cloth, 5s.

HOOK'S PROPER NAMES IN HOLY SCRIPTURE ACCENTED. 1s.

COTTON'S OBSOLETE WORDS IN THE BIBLE. 6d.

JONES (of Nayland) ON THE FIGURATIVE LANGUAGE OF HOLY SCRIPTURE. Cloth, 1s. 6d.

THE RIGHT WAY OF READING SCRIPTURE. From the Parochial Tracts. 18 for 1s.

A FIRST CATECHISM OF THE BIBLE. By ARCHDEACON FFOULKES. Second Edition. 18mo., 6d.

THOUGHTS ON THE WORK OF THE SIX DAYS OF CREATION. By J. W. BOWDEN, M.A. Fcap. 8vo., cloth, 2s. 6d.

SACRIFICE THE DIVINE SERVICE. By J. SCANDRET. 18mo., cloth, 2s. 6d.

OXFORD, AND 377, STRAND, LONDON.

THE HOLY SCRIPTURES (*continued*).

The Psalms.

A PLAIN COMMENTARY ON THE BOOK OF PSALMS (Prayer-book Version), chiefly grounded on the Fathers. For the Use of Families. 2 vols., Fcap. 8vo., cloth, 10s. 6d.

PAROCHIAL LECTURES ON THE PSALMS, from the Fathers of the Primitive Church. By the Rev. F. H. Dunwell, B.A., Curate of Glooston. 8vo., cloth, 6s.

THE PSALTER AND THE GOSPEL. The Life, Sufferings, and Triumph of Our Blessed Lord, revealed in the Book of Psalms. Fcap. 8vo., cl., 3s.

KEY WORDS TO THE PSALTER; being Short Anthems, or Antiphons, proper to each Psalm. Reprinted from the "Penny Post." 8vo., 8d. each.

The Prophets.

THE PROPHECIES OF ISAIAH. Their Authenticity and Messianic Interpretation Vindicated, in a Course of Sermons preached before the University of Oxford. By the Rev. R. Payne Smith, D.D., Regius Professor of Divinity, (Dean of Canterbury). 8vo., cloth, 10s. 6d.

DANIEL THE PROPHET. Nine Lectures delivered in the Divinity School of the University of Oxford. By the Rev. E. B. Pusey, D.D., Regius Professor of Hebrew in the University of Oxford. With Copious Notes. Third Edition. Sixth Thousand. 8vo., cloth, 10s. 6d.

THE MINOR PROPHETS; with a Commentary Explanatory and Practical, and Introductions to the Several Books. By the Rev. E. B. Pusey, D.D. 4to., sewed, 6s. each part.

Part I. contains Hosea—Joel, Introduction.
Part II. Joel, Introduction—Amos vi. 6.
Part III. Amos vi. 7 to Micah i. 17.
Part IV. Micah i. 18 to Habakkuk, Introduction.
Part V. Habakkuk, Ephraim, Haggai. (In preparation.

LIBRI ENOCH PROPHETÆ VERSIO ÆTHIOPICA, quam secuti sub fine novissimi ex Abyssinia Britanniam Advecta vix Tandem Litterata Orbis Innotuit; edita a Ricardo Laurence, LL.D., Archiepiscopo Camilleusi. 8vo., cloth, 7s. 6d.

St. Paul's Epistles.

CHRISTIANITY AS TAUGHT BY S. PAUL. By William J. Irons, D.D., of Queen's College, Oxford; Prebendary of S. Paul's; being the BAMPTON LECTURES for the year 1870, with an Appendix of the Contiguous Sense of S. Paul's Epistles; with Notes and Metalegomena. 8vo., cloth, with Map, 14s.

ST. PAUL'S EPISTLES TO THE EPHESIANS AND PHILIPPIANS, A Practical and Exegetical Commentary. Edited by the late Rev. Henry Newland. 8vo., cloth, 7s. 6d.

REFLECTIONS IN A LENT READING OF THE EPISTLE TO THE ROMANS. By the late Rev. C. Marriott. Fcap. 8vo., cloth, 3s.

THE HOLY SCRIPTURES (*continued*).

The Four Gospels.

THE CATENA AUREA. A Commentary on the Four Gospels, collected out of the Works of the Fathers by S. Thomas Aquinas. Uniform with the Library of the Fathers. Re-issue, 6 vols., cloth, £2 2s.

A PLAIN COMMENTARY ON THE FOUR HOLY GOSPELS, intended chiefly for Devotional Reading. By the Rev. J. W. Burgon, B.D., Vicar of St. Mary's, Oxford, and Gresham Lecturer in Divinity. New Edition. 6 vols., Fcap. 8vo., limp cloth, £1 1s.

SAYINGS ASCRIBED TO OUR LORD by the Fathers and other Primitive Writers, and Incidents in His Life narrated by them, otherwise than found in Scripture. By John Theodore Dodd, B.A., late Student of Christ Church, Oxford. Fcap. 8vo., cloth, 3s.

THE LAST TWELVE VERSES OF THE GOSPEL ACCORDING TO S. MARK, Vindicated against Recent Critical Objectors and Established, by John W. Burgon, B.D. With Facsimiles of Codex ℵ and Codex L. 8vo., cloth, 12s.

THE GOSPELS FROM A RABBINICAL POINT OF VIEW, shewing the perfect Harmony of the Four Evangelists on the subject of our Lord's Last Supper, and the Bearing of the Laws and Customs of the Jews at the time of our Lord's coming on the Language of the Gospels. By the Rev. G. Wilson Pearitt, M.A. Crown 8vo., limp cloth, 3s.

THE FOUR GOSPELS AND THE ACTS OF THE APOSTLES arranged in Paragraphs, with Short Notes for the Use of Schools. By Henry Cotton, D.C.L., Archdeacon of Cashel. Fcap. 8vo., roan, 3s.

LECTURES, EXPLANATORY OF THE DIATESSARON; or, The History of our Lord and Saviour Jesus Christ, collected from the Four Gospels, in the form of a Continuous Narrative. By John David Macbride, D.C.L. Fifth Edition. 2 vols., 8vo., cloth, 12s.

HARMONISED SUMMARY OF THE GOSPELS. By J. James. 8vo., 4d.

OUR LORD'S MIRACLES OF HEALING considered in relation to Medical Science, &c. By T. W. Belcher, M.D., M.A. Crown 8vo., cloth, 2s. 6d.

SHORT NOTES ON ST. JOHN'S GOSPEL. For the Use of Teachers in Parish Schools. By Downing. Fcap. 8vo., cloth, 2s. 6d.

A HARMONY OF THE GOSPELS, from "Daily Steps." 32mo., 2d.

PARABLES AND MIRACLES. See "Catechetical Lessons" on page 40.

The Acts of the Apostles.

LECTURES ON THE ACTS OF THE APOSTLES, AND ON THE EPISTLES. By John David Macbride, D.C.L., Principal of Magdalen Hall, Oxford. 8vo., cloth, 10s. 6d.

SHORT NOTES ON THE ACTS OF THE APOSTLES. By Henry Downing, M.A. Uniform with the above. Fcap. 8vo., cloth, 2s.

AN ATTEMPT TO ASCERTAIN THE CHRONOLOGY OF THE ACTS OF THE APOSTLES, &c. By E. Burton, D.D., Regius Professor of Divinity. 8vo., 2s. 6d.

The Prayer-book.

THE PRINCIPLES OF DIVINE SERVICE; or, An Inquiry concerning the True Manner of Understanding and Using the Order for Morning and Evening Prayer, and for the Administration of the Holy Communion in the English Church. By the Rev. Philip Freeman, M.A., Vicar of Thorverton, and Archdeacon of Exeter, &c. 2 vols., 8vo., cloth, 16s.

A HISTORY OF THE BOOK OF COMMON PRAYER, and other Authorized Books, from the Reformation; and an Attempt to ascertain how the Rubrics, Canons, and Customs of the Church have been understood and observed from the same time. By the Rev. T. Lathbury, M.A. Second Edition. 8vo., cloth, 10s. 6d.

CATECHETICAL LESSONS ON THE BOOK OF COMMON PRAYER. Illustrating the Prayer-book, from its Title-page to the end of the Collects, Epistles, and Gospels. Designed to aid the Clergy in Public Catechising. By the Rev. Dr. Francis Hessey, Incumbent of St. Barnabas, Kensington. Fcap. 8vo., cloth, 6s.

A COMPANION TO THE PRAYER-BOOK. Compiled from the best Sources. 18mo., limp cloth, 1s.

The Lord's Prayer.

AN EXPOSITION OF THE LORD'S PRAYER, Devotional, Doctrinal, and Practical; with four Preliminary Dissertations, &c. By the Rev. W. H. Karslake, Fellow and sometime Tutor of Merton College, Oxford. 8vo., cloth, 7s. 6d.

The Epistles and Gospels.

A COMMENTARY ON THE EPISTLES AND GOSPELS IN THE BOOK OF COMMON PRAYER. Extracted from Writings of the Fathers of the Holy Catholic Church, anterior to the Division of the East and West. By a Lay Member of the Church. With an Introductory Notice by the Dean of St. Paul's. In Four Parts. Part I. Advent—Quinquagesima. Crown 8vo., paper covers, 3s. Part II., *in the Press.*

The Ordination Service.

ADDRESSES TO THE CANDIDATES FOR ORDINATION ON THE QUESTIONS IN THE ORDINATION SERVICE. By the late Samuel Wilberforce, D.D., Lord Bishop of Winchester, Prelate of the Most Noble Order of the Garter. Sixth Thousand. Crown 8vo., cloth, 6s.

For Minor Works on the Church Catechism, Baptism, Confirmation, &c., see Parochial, pp. 40, 41.

Ecclesiastical History, &c.

A History of the Church,
From the Edict of Milan, A.D. 813, to the Council of Chalcedon, A.D. 451. By WILLIAM BRIGHT, D.D., Regius Professor of Ecclesiastical History, and Canon of Christ Church, Oxford. Second Edition. Post 8vo., 10s. 6d.

Manual of Ecclesiastical History,
From the First to the Twelfth Century inclusive. By the Rev. E. S. PROULEES, M.A., Fellow and Tutor of Jesus College, Oxford. 8vo., cloth, 6s.

The Age of the Martyrs;
Or, The First Three Centuries of the Work of the Church of our Lord and Saviour Jesus Christ. By JOHN DAVID JENKINS, B.D., Fellow of Jesus College, Oxford; Canon of Pieter Maritzburg. Crown 8vo., cloth, 6s.

The Councils of the Church,
From the Council of Jerusalem to the close of the Second General Council of Constantinople, A.D. 381. By the Rev. E. B. PUSEY, D.D. 1857. 8vo., 10s. 6d.

The Ecclesiastical History of the First Three Centuries,
From the Crucifixion of Jesus Christ to the year 313. By the late Rev. Dr. BURTON. Fourth Edition. 8vo., cloth, 12s.

A Brief History of the Christian Church,
From the First Century to the Reformation. By the Rev. J. S. BARTLETT. Fcap. 8vo., cloth, 2s. 6d.

History of the so-called Jansenist Church of Holland;
With a Sketch of its Earlier Annals, and some Account of the Brothers of the Common Life. By the late Rev. J. M. NEALE, Warden of Sackville College. 8vo., cloth, 6s.

A History of the English Church,
From its Foundation to the Reign of Queen Mary. Addressed to the Young. By M. C. S. Crown 8vo., cloth, 5s.

Bede's Ecclesiastical History of the English Nation.
A New Translation by the Rev. L. GIDLEY, M.A., Chaplain of St. Nicholas', Salisbury. Crown 8vo., cloth, 6s.

OXFORD, AND 377, STRAND, LONDON.

ECCLESIASTICAL HISTORY (*continued*).

St. Paul in Britain;

Or, The Origin of British as Opposed to Papal Christianity. By the Rev. R.
W. Morgan. Crown 8vo., cloth, 3s.

Peter the Apostle never at Rome,

Shewn to be a Historical Fact; with a Dissertation of the Apostolic Authority
of the Symbol (or Creed) of the Church. By J. H. Brown, M.A., Rector
of Middleton-in-Teesdale. Post 8vo., limp cloth, 2s. 6d.

The Sufferings of the Clergy

During the Great Rebellion. By the Rev. John Walker, M.A., sometime of
Exeter College, Oxford, and Rector of St. Mary Major, Exeter. Epitomised
by the Author of "The Annals of England." Fcap. 8vo., cloth, 5s.

Scotland and the Scottish Church.

By the Rev. H. Caswall, M.A., Vicar of Figheldean, Wilts.; Author of
"America and the American Church," &c. Fcap. 8vo., cloth, 2s. 6d.

Fasti Ecclesiæ Hibernicæ.

The Succession of the Prelates and Members of the Cathedral Bodies in Ireland. By Henry Cotton, D.C.L., Archdeacon of Cashel. Vols. I. to IV.,
8vo., cloth, £2 10s.; Vol. V., 8vo., cloth, 10s. 6d.

The Church.

By Frances Parker, M.A., Trinity College, Cambridge; Presbyter of the
Diocese of Exeter, &c. With a Chart. Folio, cloth, £3 3s.

THREE INTRODUCTORY LEC-
TURES ON THE STUDY OF
ECCLESIASTICAL HISTORY.
By Arthur Penrhyn Stanley,
D.D., Dean of Westminster. 8vo.,
3s. 6d.

THE CROSS AND THE SER-
PENT: Being a Brief History of
the Triumph of the Cross, through
a long Series of Ages, in Prophecy,
Type, and Fulfilment. By the
Rev. W. Haslam, Perpetual Curate
of S. Michael's, Baldhu. 12mo.,
cloth, 5s.

THE EMPIRE and the CHURCH,
from Constantine to Charlemagne.
By Mrs. Hamilton Gray. Post
8vo., cloth, 12s.

THE WESTERN WORLD RE-
VISITED. By the Rev. Henry
Caswall, M.A., Vicar of Fighel-
dean. Fcap. 8vo., cloth, 3s.

JOURNAL OF A RESIDENCE
AT THE COLLEGE OF ST. CO-
LUMBA IN IRELAND. With a
Preface. By the Rev. W. Sewell,
D.D. Second Edition. 12mo.,
cloth, 4s

Library of the Fathers

OF THE HOLY CATHOLIC CHURCH, ANTERIOR TO THE
DIVISION OF THE EAST AND WEST.

*Translated by Members of the English Church, and Edited by the
Rev. R. B. PUSEY, D.D.*

Subscribers' price.

	£	s.	d.
St. Augustine's Confessions. 3rd Edit. 8vo., cloth, 9s.	0	7	0
——— Sermons. Vol. I. 2nd Edit. 14s.	} 1	1	0
——— Sermons. Vol. II. *Reprinting.*			
——— Homilies on the Psalms. Vol. I. 10s. 6d.			
——— on the Psalms. Vol. II. 10s. 6d.			
——— on the Psalms. Vol. III. 14s.			
——— on the Psalms. Vol. IV. 14s.	} 2	16	0
——— on the Psalms. Vol. V. 12s.			
——— on the Psalms. Vol. VI. 14s.			
——— on St. John. Vol. I. 14s.	} 1	2	6
——— on St. John. Vol. II. 16s.			
——— Short Treatises. 16s.	0	12	0
St. Athanasius against the Arians. Part I. 9s.	} 0	15	0
——— against the Arians. Part II. 2nd Edit. 10s. 6d.			
——— Historical Tracts. 2nd Edit. 10s. 6d.	0	8	0
——— Festal Epistles. 6s.	0	4	6
St. Chrysostom's Homilies on St. Matthew. Part I. 12s.			
——— on St. Matthew. Part II. 12s.	} 1	7	0
——— on St. Matthew. Part III. 12s.			
——— on St. John. Vol. I. 10s. 6d.	} 0	18	6
——— on St. John. Part II. 14s.			
——— on the Acts. Part I. 10s. 6d.	} 0	16	0
——— on the Acts. Part II. 10s. 6d.			
——— on Romans. *Reprinting.*			
——— on 1 Corinthians. 2 vols. 18s.	0	14	0
——— on 2 Corinthians. 10s. 6d.	0	8	0
——— on Galatians and Ephesians. *Reprinting.*			
——— on Philippians, &c. *Reprinting.*			
——— on Timothy, Titus, and Philemon. 12s.	0	9	0
——— on the Statues. 12s.	0	9	0
St. Cyprian's Treatises. 2nd Edit. 10s. 6d.	} 0	17	0
——— Epistles. 12s.			
St. Cyril (of Jerusalem). Lectures. 3rd Edit. 10s. 6d.	0	8	0
St. Cyril (of Alexandria), on St. John. *Vol. I. nearly ready.*			
——— Five Books against Nestorius, &c. *In preparation.*			
St. Ephrem's Rhythms (from the Syriac). 14s.	0	10	6
St. Gregory the Great, Morals on Job. Vol. I. 15s.			
——— Morals, etc. Vol. II. 15s.	} 2	2	0
——— Morals, etc. Vol. III. Part I. 10s. 6d.			
——— Morals, etc. Vol. III. Part II. 15s.			
St. Irenæus, Works of. 14s.	0	10	6
St. Justin Martyr, Works of. 8s.	0	6	0
Tertullian, Treatises. 2nd Edit. 15s.	0	11	0

OXFORD, AND 377, STRAND, LONDON.

The Library of the Fathers.

THE ORIGINAL TEXTS.

Edited by the Rev. E. B. PUSEY, D.D.

	Subscribers' price.
	£ s. d.
ST. AUGUSTINI Confessiones (revised with the use of some Oxford MSS. and early editions) . .	0 7 0
ST. CHRYSOSTOMI in Epist. ad Romanos . .	0 9 0
———————— ad Corinthios I. . .	0 10 6
———————— ad Corinthios II. . .	0 8 0
———————— ad Galatas et Ephesios .	0 7 0
———————— ad Phil., Coloss., Thessal. .	0 10 6
———————— ad Tim., Tit., Philem. .	0 6 0
———————— ad Hebraeos . . .	0 9 0

(For this edition all the good MSS. of St. Chrysostom in public libraries in Europe have been collated, and the Rev. F. Field having employed his great critical acumen upon them, the English edition of St. Chrysostom is, so far, the best extant, as Sir H. Savile's was in his day.)

THEODORETI Commentarius in omnes B. Pauli Epistolas, Edidit C. MARRIOTT. Pars I. continens Epistolas ad Romanos, Corinthios, et Galatas .	0 8 0
———————— Pars II. ad Ephes., Philip., Coloss., Thess., Heb., Tim., Tit., et Philem. . .	0 6 0

To Subscribers only, 10 vols., 8vo., cloth, 12s. per volume.

A NEW EDITION OF THE WORK OF S. CYRIL, ARCHBISHOP OF ALEXANDRIA. Vols. I. and II., containing the COMMENTARIES UPON THE TWELVE MINOR PROPHETS, and Vols. III., IV., and V., containing the COMMENTARY ON S. JOHN, can be delivered to Subscribers now.

Vol. VI., containing LIBRI V. CONTRA NESTORIUM, EXPLANATIO XII. CAPITUM, DEFENSIONES XII. CAPITUM, SCHOLIA DE INCARNATIONE UNIGENITI, will be issued in the course of 1874.

Vol. VII. will be divided into two parts, the first containing the DE RECTA FIDE TRES TRACTATUS, QUOD UNUS EST CHRISTUS, DIALOGUS, APOLOGETICTS, and some few of the HOMILIES. This first half will be issued, it is hoped, early in 1875. The other half, containing the EPISTLES, will be kept till last, to allow of the most complete researches possible being made.

Vol. VIII. of the series will contain the PASCHAL HOMILIES.

Vol. IX. The Treatises DE TRINITATE AD HERMIAM, &c.

Vol. X. The THESAURUS.

Vol. VII., Part II.—EPISTLES.

The Editor cannot undertake to continue the half-yearly issue to the end of the series. After the first two years only one volume will be issued in each year. This will bring the series to a completion in 1878. It is computed that the average will be about 650 pages in each volume.

Subscribers' Names should be sent to James Parker and Co., Broad-street, Oxford, of whom Prospectuses may be obtained.

OXFORD, AND 377, STRAND, LONDON.

RE-ISSUE OF THE

Library of Anglo-Catholic Theology.

SIX VOLUMES FOR ONE GUINEA.

IN order to meet the desire of many of the Clergy to possess the writings of the chief Divines of the English Church, provided they can do so at small cost, it has been determined to commence a re-issue of the Anglo-Catholic Library, Six Volumes to be issued in each year, and at the Subscription of One Guinea.

The order of the issue will be as follows :—

1874.

ANDREWES (Lancelot, Bishop of Winchester)—Sermons, Vol. 1. Of the Nativity; of Repentance and Fasting.
——— Sermons, Vol. II. Sermons preached in Lent; of the Passion, and of the Resurrection.
WILSON (Thomas, Bishop of Sodor and Man)—Works, Vol. I., Life, Part 1.
——— Works, Vol. I., Life, Part 2.
These two volumes contain the Life of Bishop Wilson, by the Rev. J. KEBLE.
COSIN (John, Bishop of Durham)—Works, Vol. 1. Life; Sermons.
——— Works, Vol. II. Articles to be enquired of by Churchwardens and Swornmen; the Sum and Substance of the Conferences concerning Mr. Montague's Books; Private Devotions.

1875.

ANDREWES' Sermons, Vol. III. Of the Resurrection; of the Sending of the Holy Ghost.
——— Sermons, Vol. IV. Of the Conspiracy of the Gowries; of Gunpowder Treason.
WILSON's Works, Vol. II. Sermons L.—L.
——— Works, Vol. III. Sermons LI.—XCIX.
BULL (George, Bishop of S. David's)—Harmonia Apostolica. Two Dissertations; in the former of which the Doctrine of S. James on Justification by Works is explained and defended; in the latter, the agreement of S. Paul with S. James is clearly shewn.
——— Examen Censuræ: an Answer to certain Strictures on the Harmonia Apostolica, to which is added an Apology for the Harmony and its Author.

1876.

ANDREWES' Sermons, Vol. V. Miscellaneous.
——— Pattern of Catechistical Doctrine; together with Judgment of the Lambeth Articles; Form of Consecration of a Church and Churchyard; Summary View of the Government both of the Old and New Testament; Discourse of Ceremonies retained and used in Christian Churches.
BULL's Defence of the Nicene Creed, out of the Writings of the Catholic Doctors who flourished during the first three centuries of the Christian Church; in which also is incidentally vindicated the Creed of Constantinople, concerning the Holy Ghost. Vol. I.
——— Defence of the Nicene Creed, Vol. II.
COSIN's Works, Vol. III. A Scholastical History of the Canon of the Holy Scripture.
——— Works, Vol. IV. Miscellaneous Works, including the Historia Transubstantiationis, with Luke de Beaulieu's Translation.

OXFORD, AND 377, STRAND, LONDON.

LIBRARY OF ANGLO-CATHOLIC THEOLOGY (*continued*).

1877.

ANDREWES' Minor Works, including the Life, by Isaacson; two Answers to Cardinal Perron, &c.; Manual for the Sick; Manual of Private Devotions, &c.; with Indices.

COSIN'S Works, Vol. V. Notes and Collections on the Book of Common Prayer.

JOHNSON (John)—The Unbloody Sacrifice and Altar, unvailed and supported; in which the nature of the Eucharist is explained according to the Sentiments of the English Church in the first four Centuries. Vol. I.

——— Unbloody Sacrifice, Vol. II.

WILSON'S Works, Vol. IV. Instructions for such as have learned the Church Catechism; an Instruction for the Indians; a Short Introduction to the Lord's Supper.

——— Works, Vol. V. Sacra Privata; Supplement to Sacra Privata; Maxims of Piety; Supplement to Maxims of Piety.

1878.

WILSON'S Works, Vol. VI. Notes on the Holy Scriptures.

——— Works, Vol. VII. Parochialia; with other Tracts and Fragments, and a General Index.

JOHNSON'S Collection of the Laws and Canons of the Church of England. Translated into English, with Explanatory Notes. Vol. I. From its first Foundation to the Conquest.

——— Laws and Canons, Vol. II. From the Conquest to the Reign of King Henry VIII.

BULL'S Judgment of the Catholic Church on the necessity of believing that our Lord Jesus Christ is very God; the Primitive and Apostolic Tradition of the Doctrine concerning the Divinity of our Saviour Jesus Christ; Brief Animadversions on a Treatise of Mr. Gilbert Clerke.

L'ESTRANGE (Hamon)—The Alliance of Divine Offices, exhibiting all the Liturgies of the Church of England since the Reformation; as also the late Scotch Service-book, with all their respective Variations; with Annotations.

At the close of the first five years the English works of Bishops Andrewes, Wilson, and Cosin, and of Bull, Johnson, and L'Estrange (so far as they appear in the Anglo-Catholic Library) will be complete. The next five years will comprise the complete English Works of Beveridge, Bramhall, Hammond, and Laud, with one or two minor works.

Subscribers to the first five years' issue are in no wise bound to continue their subscription to the next five, and hence arrangements have been made that the works of the several authors should be completed before the Second Series was commenced.

The Publishers will close the Subscription List when the names sent in exceed in number the copies they have in stock of those volumes which they do not judge it expedient to reprint. Several of the volumes are now in course of being reprinted.

Those volumes only which belong to the year for which the subscription is paid will be delivered for that subscription.

Subscriptions will be due on the 1st of January each year, beginning 1874. On receipt of subscription, the six volumes will be immediately sent; or should the subscription list be closed, the remittance will be at once returned.

LIBRARY OF ANGLO-CATHOLIC THEOLOGY (*continued*).

The following Works were also issued originally in the Anglo - Catholic Library. Only a few copies remain of some of the volumes.

LANCELOT ANDREWES, D.D., LATIN WORKS.

	£	s.	d.
Tortura Torti . . . ;	0	6	0
Responsio ad Apologiam Card. Bellarmini . . .	0	6	0
Preces Privatæ Quotidianæ. Gr. et Lat. . .	0	5	0
Opuscula Posthuma et Index in Opera Latina . .	0	4	0

The Works of Bp. Andrewes complete, with Life and Indices, 11 Volumes. Price Three Pounds Seven Shillings.

WILLIAM BEVERIDGE, D.D., Bishop of St. Asaph.

The English Theological Works. 10 vols. . . .	3	10	0
Codex Canonum. 2 vols	0	14	0

Works complete, 12 Volumes. Price Four Guineas.

(N.B. The Volumes may be had separately, to complete sets, at 7s. each.)

Volumes 1 to 6 contain Sermons. Vol. 7, On the Thirty-Nine Articles. Vol. 8, The Church Catechism explained ; Private Thoughts on Religion ; Of Public Prayer, &c. ; Defence of the Book of Psalms, (Old Version.) Vols. 9 and 10, Thesaurus Theologicus. Vols. 11 and 12, Codex Canonum Ecclesiæ Primitivæ Vindicatus ac Illustratus.

JOHN BRAMHALL, D.D., Archbishop of Armagh.

The Works, with Life and Letters, &c. 5 vols . .	1	15	0

(N.B. Vols. 1, 2, 4, 5, may be had separately, price 7s. each Volume.)

.The 5 Volumes, amongst many other matters, include—A Life of the Author ; Several Sermons, Letters, &c ; A Vindication of the Church of England from the Aspersion of Criminal Schism ; The Consecration of Protestant Bishops Vindicated and Nag's Head Fable refuted ; Fair Warning of Scotch Discipline ; Vindication of Himself and Episcopal Clergy from charge of Popery ; Defence of True Liberty against Mr. Hobbes.

RICHARD CRAKANTHORP, [Born 1567, dec. 1624.]

Defensio Ecclesiæ Anglicanæ	0	7	0

MARK FRANK, D.D., [Born 1613, dec. 1664.]

The Sermons. 2 vols.	0	10	0

WILLIAM FORBES, D.D., [Bishop of Edinburgh.]

Considerationes Modestæ. 2 vols.	0	12	0

Vol. 1 contains De Justificatione. Vol. 2. De Purgatorio, Invocatione Sanctorum, Christo Mediatore, et Eucharistia. Vita Authoris, &c.

BRARY OF ANGLO-CATHOLIC THEOLOGY (*continued*).

	£	s.	d.

PETER GUNNING, D.D., [Born 1613, dec. 1684.]
Paschal, or Lent Fast 0 6 0

HENRY HAMMOND, D.D., [Born 1605, dec. 1660.]
ractical Catechism 0 5 0
sellaneous Theological Works 0 5 0
ty-one Sermons, 2 Parts 0 10 0

GEORGE HICKES, D.D., [Born 1642, dec. 1715.]
Treatises on the Christian Priesthood. 3 vols. . 0 15 0

WILLIAM LAUD, D.D., Archbishop of Canterbury.
Works complete. 7 vols., 8vo. (9 Parts) . . 2 17 0

I. I. contains Sermons on several occasions. VOL. II. Conference with Fisher,
published 1609), VOL. III. Summary of Devotions. Diary of the Arch-
p's Life. Notes on Prynne's Breviate. History of Troubles and Trial.
IV. Troubles and Trial (continued). The Archbishop's Dying Speech.
mi Will and Testament. Rome's Masterpiece. VOL. V. Parts I. and II.
ry of his Chancellorship of the University of Oxford, &c. Accounts of
Provisions, Constitutions and Canons. VOL. VI. Parts I. and II. Several
vr hitherto unpublished, &c. Miscellaneous Papers. Letters. Notes on
calms. VOL. VII. Letters.

NATHANIEL MARSHALL, D.D., Born Dec. 1730-1.
Penitential Discipline 0 4 0

WILLIAM NICHOLSON, D.D., Bishop of Gloucester.
Exposition of the Catechism 0 6 0

BISHOP OVERALL, Born 1559, dec. 1619.
Convocation-Book of 1606. 8vo. . . . 0 5 0

JOHN PEARSON, D.D., Bishop of Chester.
llcise Epistolarum S. Ignatii. 2 vols. . . . 0 10 0

HERBERT THORNDIKE, [born 1598, dec. 1672.]
Theological Works complete. 6 vols. (10 Parts) 2 10 0

e Volumes contain, among other matters:—VOL. I. (2 Parts) Of the
rument of Churches. Of Religious Assemblies, and the Public Service of
The Rights of the Church in a Christian State. VOL. II. (2 Parts) The
iples of Christian Truth. VOL. III. (2 Parts) The Covenant of Grace.
IV. (2 Parts) The Laws of the Church. VOL. V. The present state of Re-
amongst us. Due way of composing Differences. Just Weights and Mea-
. True Principle of Comprehension.—Plea of Weakness and Tender Con-
us. Of the Forbearance of Penalties, &c. Reformation of the Church of
ind. VOL. VI. The Church's Right to Tithes, &c. The Church's Power of
ommunication, &c. The Church's Legislative Power, &c. Rights of the
tian State in Church Matters. Letters and Papers. Life. Index.

Sermons.

ABRAHAM.—Festival and Lenten Lectures, delivered at St. George's Chapel, Windsor, with special reference to the Ecclesiastical and Social Questions of the Day, in 1848-9. By the Right Rev. C. J. ABRAHAM, D.D., late Bishop of Wellington. 8vo., cloth, 5s.

ALLEGORICAL SERMONS.—Short Allegorical Sermons. CONTENTS: 1. The City of the Lost; 2. The Prisoner of Hope; 3. The Soldier; 4. The Hounds; 5. The Slaves; 6. The Stone of Reparation; 7. The Stranger; 8. The Unnatural Sentence; 9. The Guestchamber; 10. The Exile; 11. The Three Fields; 12. The Bargain. Third Edition. Fcap. 8vo., toned paper, cloth, 2s.

ARMSTRONG. — Parochial Sermons. By JOHN ARMSTRONG, D.D., late Lord Bishop of Grahamstown. Fifth Edition. Fcap. 8vo., cl., 5s.

——— Sermons on the Fasts and Festivals. Third Edition. Fcap. 8vo., cloth, 5s.

BARKER.—Plain Sermons preached in Parish Churches. By THOMAS BARKER, M.A., of Queen's College, Oxford, &c. Post 8vo., cloth, 6s.

BENTLEY.—Sermons on Atheism, by R. BENTLEY. 8vo., cloth, 4s.

BERNARD.—The Witness of God: Five Sermons preached before the University of Oxford. By THOMAS DEHANY BERNARD, M.A. Exeter College; Rector of Walcot; one of the Select Preachers for 1855-6, and 1862-3; Bampton Lecturer for 1864. Crown 8vo., cloth, 8s.

BEVERIDGE. — Sermons on the Ministry and Ordinances of the Church of England. By Bishop BEVERIDGE. 12mo., cloth, 3s.

BOYLE.—How and for What we ought to Pray; a Series of Eight Lectures on the Lord's Prayer, &c. By the Rev. JOHN BOYLE, Incumbent of Stramshall. Fcap. 8vo., cloth, 3s. 6d.

BULL.—Jesus and the Twelve; or, The Training by Christ of His Disciples. By the Rev. A. H. BULL, M.A., Incumbent of Corse Abbas. Post 8vo., cloth, 5s.

BURGON.—Ninety Short Sermons for Family Reading, following the Order of the Christian Seasons. By the Rev. J. W. BURGON, M.A., Vicar of St. Mary's, Oxford. 2 vols., Fcap. 8vo., 8s.

——— Ditto. Second Series. 2 vols., Fcap. 8vo., 8s.

BURROWS. — Parochial Sermons, by the Rev. HENRY W. BURROWS, B.D., Perpetual Curate of Christ Church, St. Pancras. Second Series. Fcap. 8vo., cloth, 5s.

BURTON.—Sermons on the Offices for the Visitation of the Sick, and the Burial of the Dead. By CHAS. JAMES BURTON, M.A., Chancellor of Carlisle, and Vicar of Lydd. Post 8vo., cloth, 3s. 6d.

CHRISTIAN SEASONS, Sermons for. See page 36.

CURTEIS. — Spiritual Progress: Four Sermons preached in the Chapel of Exeter College, Oxford. By G. H. CURTEIS, M.A., Fellow and Catechist. Fcap. 8vo., cl., 2s.

FRASER.—Six Sermons preached before the University of Oxford. By the Right Rev. JAMES FRASER, D.D., Bishop of Manchester. Fcap. 8vo., cloth, 3s. 6d.

FRASER.—Parish Sermons. Second Series. By WILLIAM FRASER, D.C.L., Vicar of Alton. Fcap. 8vo., cloth, 2s. 6d.

FURSE.—Sermons preached for the most part in the Churches of St. Mary and St. Matthias, Richmond, Surrey. By CHARLES W. FURSE, M.A., Principal of Cuddesdon Theological College. Post 8vo., cl., 6s.

HARRIS.—Historical Religion, and Biblical Revelation. By HENRY HARRIS, B.D., Rector of Winterbourne Bassett. Crown 8vo, cloth, 3s. 6d.

SERMONS (*continued*).

HARRIS.—The Baptismal Covenant. Eight Lectures addressed chiefly to Candidates for Confirmation, in the Church of Tor Mohun, Torquay. By J. H. HARRIS, D.D., Perpetual Curate. Fcap. 8vo., cloth, 2s. 6d.

HARSTON.—Sermons by the Rev. EDWARD HARSTON, M.A., Vicar and Rural Dean of Tamworth. 8vo., cloth, 10s. 6d.

HEATHCOTE. — Seven Sermons preached during Lent and Easter. Post 8vo., limp cloth, 2s. 6d.

HEATHCOTE.—Sermons. By GIL-BERT VYVYAN HEATHCOTE, Lite-rate Priest; Perpetual Curate of Hopton Cangeford, Rector of Herr-ford; Author of "Seven Sermons," &c. Crown 8vo., cloth, 5s.

BEURTLEY.—Sermons on some Subjects of Recent Controversy, preached before the University of Oxford. 1. Outward Observances. 2. The Eucharistic Sacrifice. 3. The Better Covenant. 4. The Shiloh. 5. Summary View of the Christian Evidences. By CHAS. A. HEURT-LEY, D.D., Margaret Professor of Divinity, and Canon of Christ Church. 8vo., cloth, 5s.

——— The Union between Christ and His People. Four Sermons preached before the University of Oxford. By CHARLES A. HEURTLEY, D.D. 8vo., cloth, 5s. 6d.

HUNTINGTON.—Sermons for the Holy Seasons of the Church. AD-VENT TO TRINITY. By GEORGE HUNTINGTON, M.A., Rector of Tenby, &c. Second Edition. Crown 8vo., cloth, 5s.

HUNTLEY. — The Year of the Church. A Course of Sermons by the late Rev. RICHARD WEBSTER HUNTLEY, M.A., sometime Fellow of All Souls College, Oxford, &c.; with a short Memoir by the Editor, the Rev. SIR G. PREVOST, Bart., M.A. Fcap. 8vo., cloth, 7s. 6d.

JACOBSON.—Sermons preached in the Parish Church of Iffley, Oxon. By the Right Rev. WILLIAM JACOB-SON, D.D., Bishop of Chester. Se-cond Edition. Crown 8vo., cloth, 6s.

JELF.—Twelve Sermons preached at the Chapel Royal, Whitehall. By WILLIAM EDWARD JELF, B.D., Senior Censor of Christ Church, and late Whitehall Preacher. 8vo., cloth, 7s. 6d.

KEBLE.—Village Sermons on the Baptismal Service. By the Rev. JOHN KEBLE, M.A., Author of "The Christian Year." 8vo., cloth, 6s.

KEBLE—Sermons Occasional and Parochial. By the Rev. JOHN KEBLE, M.A. 8vo., cloth, 12s.

KEBLE.—Sermons, Academical and Occasional. By the Rev. JOHN KEBLE, M.A. 8vo., cloth, 12s.

KENNAWAY.—Some Tones of the Voice of Prophecy, and of the Voice of Miracle. By the Rev. C. E. KENNAWAY, M.A., Vicar of Campden. With an Introduction by the Right Rev. SAMUEL WIL-BERFORCE, Bishop of Oxford. Crown 8vo., cloth, 5s.

LENTEN SERMONS AT OX-FORD.—The Series for 1858. Fcap. 8vo., cloth, 5s.
——— The Series for 1863. 8vo., cloth, 7s. 6d.
——— The Series for 1865. 8vo., cloth, 7s. 6d.
——— The Series for 1866. 8vo., cloth, 7s. 6d.
——— The Series for 1867. 8vo., cloth, 7s. 6d.
——— The Series for 1868. 8vo., cloth, 5s.
——— The Series for 1869, 8vo., cloth, 7s. 6d.

MANNING.—Sermons preached be-fore the University of Oxford, by HENRY EDWARD MANNING, M.A., Archdeacon of Chichester, 8vo., cloth, 6s.

MANT.—Sermons for Parochial Use. By the Right Rev. R. MANT, Bishop of Down and Connor, 2 vols., 8vo., cloth, 6s.

SERMONS (continued).

MANT.—Academical Sermons. By
the Right Rev. R. MANT, Bishop of
Down and Connor, 8vo., cloth, 5s.

MARRIOTT. — Sermons preached
before the University of Oxford,
and in other places. By the late
Rev. C. MARRIOTT, Fellow of Oriel
College, Oxford. 12mo., cloth, 3s.;
also Vol. II., cloth, 3s.

MATURIN.—Six Lectures on the
Events of Holy Week. By WIL-
LIAM MATURIN, M.A., Perpetual
Curate of Grangegorman, Dublin.
Second Edition, Crown 8vo., limp
cloth, 2s. 6d.

MEYRICK.—The Wisdom of Piety,
and other Sermons, addressed chiefly
to Undergraduates. By the Rev.
FREDERICK MEYRICK, M.A., Fellow
of Trinity College, Oxford. Post
8vo., cloth, 4s.

MOBERLY.—Sermons on the Bea-
titudes, with others; mostly preached
before the University of Oxford;
with a Preface. By GEORGE MO-
BERLY, D.C.L., Bishop of Salisbury.
Third Edition. 8vo., 7s. 6d.

MONRO.—Sermons, chiefly on the
Responsibilities of the Ministerial
Office. By the late Rev. EDWARD
MONRO, Incumbent of Harrow
Weald. 8vo., cloth, 7s.

—— Illustrations of Faith. Eight
Plain Sermons: — Abel; Enoch;
Noah; Abraham; Isaac, Jacob,
and Joseph; Moses; The Walls of
Jericho; Conclusions. Fcap. 8vo.,
cloth, 3s. 6d.

—— Plain Sermons on the Book of
Common Prayer. Fcap. 8vo., cl., 5s.

—— Historical and Practical Sermons
on the Sufferings and Resurrection
of our Lord. 2 vols., Fcap. 8vo.,
cloth, 10s.

—— Sermons on New Testament
Characters. Fcap. 8vo., 4s.

MONSELL.—The Temporal Punishment of Sin, and other Sermons.
By CHARLES HENRY MONSELL,
M.A., Prebendary of Donough-
more. 18mo., cloth, 6s.

NORMAN.—Sermons preached at
St. Peter's College, Radley. By the
Rev. R. W. NORMAN, M.A., War-
den. Post 8vo., cloth, 7s. 6d.

PUSEY.—Sermons by Rev. E. B.
PUSEY, D.D. See p. 23, 24.

RICE.—Sermons preached in the
Chapel of St. Columba's College.
By CHARLES H. RICE, M.A., Vicar-
Choral of Armagh Cathedral. Crown
8vo., cloth, 5s.

SEWELL.—A Year's Sermons to
Boys, preached in the Chapel of
St. Peter's College, Radley. By
WILLIAM SEWELL, B.D., late War-
den, Vol. I, 8vo., cl, 7s. 6d.; Vol. II.,
8vo., cloth, 7s. 6d.

STANLEY.—Sermons and Essays on
the Apostolical Age. By the Very
Rev. ARTHUR PENRHYN STANLEY,
D.D., Dean of Westminster.
[A New Edition in the Press.

TRENCH.—The Salt of the Earth.
God sitting as a Refiner. Two Sermons preached at Ordinations of
the Lord Bishop of Oxford. By
RICHARD CHENEVIX TRENCH, D.D.,
Archbishop of Dublin. Fcap. 8vo.,
limp cloth, 1s. 6d.

TUPPER.—Ten Sermons in Illustration of the Creed. By the Rev. WIL-
LIAM GEORGE TUPPER, M.A., Warden of the House of Charity, Soho.
Fcap. 8vo., cloth, 3s.

WILBERFORCE. — Sermons
preached before the University of
Oxford: Third Series, 1868 to 1870.
By SAMUEL, LORD BISHOP OF WIN-
CHESTER, Prelate of the Most Noble
Order of the Garter. 8vo., cl., 7s. 6d.
—— Second Series, 1847 to 1868.
8vo., cloth, 10s. 6d.

WILLIAMS. — Sermons preached
before the University of Oxford,
and in Winchester Cathedral. By
the late DAVID WILLIAMS, D.C.L.,
Warden of New College, and Canon
of Winchester. With a brief Memoir of the Author. 8vo., cl., 10s. 6d.

YARD.—Sermons on our relation to
the Holy Trinity, and to the Church
of God. By THOMAS YARD, M.A.,
Rector of Ashwell, Rutland. Fcap.
8vo., cloth, 3s.

See also the Sermons of Andrewes,
Beveridge, Bramhall, Laud, and
Wilson in the "Library of Anglo-
Catholic Theology," pp. 16 to 19.

SERMONS (*continued*).

BY THE REV. E. B. PUSEY, D.D.

PAROCHIAL SERMONS, Vol. I., for Season from Advent to Whitsuntide.

1. The End of All Things.
2. The Merciful shall obtain Mercy.
3. Prepare for Seasons of Grace.
4. God with Us.
5. The Incarnation a Lesson of Humility.
6. Character of Christian Rebuke.
7. Joy out of Suffering.
8. God calleth thee.
9. The Presence of the Saved.
10. Fasting.
11. Review of Life.
12. Irrevocable Chastisement.
13. God's Presence in Loneliness.
14. Barabbas or Jesus.
15. Christ Risen our Justification.
16. The Christian's Life in Christ.
17. Our Risen Lord's Love for Penitents.
18. How to detain Jesus in the Soul.
19. The Christian's Life hid in Christ.
20. Increased Communions.
21. Heaven the Christian's Home.
22. The Christian the Temple of God.
22. Will of God the Care of Self-Will.

TWENTY-THREE SERMONS. 8vo., cloth, price 6s.

PAROCHIAL SERMONS, Vol. II.

1. Faith.
2. Hope.
3. Love.
4. Humility.
5. Patience.
6. Self-Knowledge.
7. Life a Warfare.
8. The Besetting Sin.
9. Victory overrides Besetting Sin.
10. Prayer heard the more through delay.
11. Re-creation of the Penitent.
12. The Sin of Judas.
13. The Ascension our Glory and Joy.
14. The Teaching of God Within and Without.
15. The Rest of Love and Praise.
16. Faith in our Lord God and Man.
17. Groans of Careless and Renewed Nature.
18. Victory amid Strife.
19. Victory through Loving Faith.
20. The Power and Greatness of Love.
21. Our Being in God.
22. The Sacrament of Marriage.

TWENTY-TWO SERMONS. 8vo., cloth, price 6s.

PAROCHIAL SERMONS, Vol. III.

Reprinted from the Plain Sermons by Contributors to the "Tracts for the Times." Revised edition.

1. Sudden Death.
2. Conversion.
3. The Cross borne for us and by us.
4. Real Obedience, in all things.
5. Christian Life a Struggle, but Victory.
6. The Value and Sacredness of Suffering.
7. The Christian's a Risen Life.
8. Victory over the World.
9. Obedience the Condition of Knowing the Truth.
10. Pray without ceasing.
11. Conditions of Acceptable Prayer.
12. Distractions in Prayer.
13. Baptism the Ground and Encouragement to Christian Education.
14. Holy Communion.—Danger in Careless Receiving.
15. Holy Communion.—Privileges.
16. Christian Kindliness and Charity.
17. Obeying Calls.
18. The Transfiguration of our Lord the Earnest of the Christian's Glory.
19. Christian Joy.
20. God's Glories in Infants set forth in the Holy Innocents.

TWENTY SERMONS. 8vo., cloth, price 6s.

PAROCHIAL SERMONS, preached and printed on Various Occasions.

1. The Day of Judgment. 9d.
2. Christ the Source and Rule of Christian Love. 1s. 6d.
3. The Preaching of the Gospel a Preparation for our Lord's Coming. 1s.
4. God is Love. 8. Whoso Receiveth One such Little Child in My Name Receiveth Me. 1s. 6d.
5. Chastisements Neglected, Forerunners of Greater. 1s.
6. The Blasphemy against the Holy Ghost. 1s.
7. Do All to the Lord Jesus. 6d.
8. The Danger of Riches.
9. Seek God First and ye shall have All. 1s. 6d.
11, 12. The Church the Converter of the Heathen. Two Sermons. 6d.
13. The Glory of God's Houses. 6d.

THIRTEEN SERMONS. 8vo., cloth, price 6s.

The above Sermons may also be had separately.

SERMONS PREACHED AT ST. SAVIOUR'S, LEEDS, On Repentance and Amendment of Life, with a Preface by Dr. Pusey.

1. Loving Penitence.
*2. The Nature of Sin.
*3. The Sinner's Death.
4. God's Merciful Visitations.
*5. The Last Judgment.
*6. Hell.
*7. Love of Christ for Penitents.
*8. The Returning Prodigal.
*9. Death to Sin in the Death of Christ.
*10. Virtue of the Cross.
11. Looking unto Jesus the Groundwork of Perseverance.
12. Looking unto Jesus the Means of Endeavour.
13. Union with Christ, &c.
14. Hopes of the Penitent.
15. Bliss of Heaven, "We shall be like Him."
16. —— "We shall see Him as He is."
17. —— Glory of the Body.
18. Progress our Perfection.
18. Daily Growth.

NINETEEN SERMONS. 8vo., cloth, price 7s. 6d.

The Sermons with an asterisk prefixed are not by Dr. Pusey.

OXFORD, AND 377, STRAND, LONDON.

SERMONS (*continued*).

BY THE REV. E. B. PUSEY, D.D.

SERMONS PREACHED BEFORE THE UNIVERSITY OF OXFORD, between a.d. 1859 and 1872.

1. Grounds of Faith difficult to analyze because Divine.
2. God is our Light in all Knowledge, Natural or Supernatural.
3. Prophecy a Series of Miracles which we can examine for ourselves.
4. The Prophecy of Christ our Atonement and Intercessor in Isaiah liii. 12.
5. The Christ the Light of the World to be rejected by His own, to be despised, and so to reign in glory.
6. Power of Truth amid Untruthfulness in Jewish Interpretation of Prophecy.
7. Causes which Blinded the Jews to the Prophecies that Jesus should suffer.
8. The Gospel could not be True unless it had certain Truth.
9. Jesus the Way, the Truth, and the Life.
10. The Doctrine of the Atonement.
11. Christ the Lord our Righteousness.
12. Human Judgment the earnest of Divine.
13. The Terror of the Day of Judgment as arising from the Justice.
14. Grieve not the Spirit of God.
15. Value of Almsgiving in the Sight of God.
16. The World an Ever-living Enemy.
17. On Human Respect.
18. Each has his own Vocation.
19. To Believe in Jesus the Teaching of the Holy Ghost.

NINETEEN SERMONS. 8vo., cloth, price 6s.

SINGLE UNIVERSITY SERMONS.

The Holy Eucharist, a Comfort for the Penitent. Preached 1843. 1s.

Entire Absolution of the Penitent. Two Sermons. Preached 1846. 1s. each.

The Presence of Christ in the Holy Eucharist. Preached 1853. 1s.

Justification. 1s.

All Faith the Gift of God. Real Faith Entire. Two Sermons. Preached 1855. 2s.

Patience and Confidence the Strength of the Church. Preached 1841. 1s.

Everlasting Punishment. Preached 1864. 6d.

Miracles of Prayer. Preached 1866. 8vo., sewed, 1s.

Will Ye also go away? Preached 1867. With Preface and Appendix. 1s.

This is My Body. Preached on the Fifth Sunday after Easter, 1871. 8vo., sewed, 1s.

The Responsibility of Intellect in Matters of Faith. Preached on Advent Sunday, 1872. With an Appendix on Bishop Moberly's Strictures on the Warning Clauses of the Athanasian Creed. 8vo., sewed, 1s.

Sinful Blindness amidst Imagined Light. Preached on the Twenty-third Sunday after Trinity, 1872. 8vo., 1s.

LENTEN SERMONS.

*Repentance from Love of God, its love. A Sermon preached in St. Mary's Church, Oxford, 1857. 1s.

*The Thought of the Love of Jesus for us the Remedy for Sins of the Body, A Sermon for Young

Men. Preached 1861. (*Second Thousand.*) 6d.

*The Spirit Comforting. Preached 1862. 1s.

Life, the Preparation for Death. A Sermon preached at Great

St. Mary's, Cambridge, 1867. 6d.

Our Pharisaism. A Sermon preached at St. Paul's, Knightsbridge, on Ash - Wednesday, 1868. 6d.

Those with an asterisk prefixed, with other Lenten Sermons, will shortly be issued in a volume.

ELEVEN ADDRESSES DURING A RETREAT OF THE COMPANIONS OF THE LOVE OF JESUS, engaged in Perpetual Intercession for the Conversion of Sinners. Eleven Sermons. 8vo., cloth, 3s. 6d.

Biographies.

REV. JOHN KEBLE.

A MEMOIR OF THE REV. JOHN KEBLE, M.A., late Vicar of Hursley. By the Right Hon. Sir J. T. COLERIDGE, D.C.L. A New and cheaper Edition. Post 8vo., cloth, 6s. [*Just ready.*

LETTERS OF SPIRITUAL COUNSEL AND GUIDANCE. By the late Rev. J. KEBLE, M.A., Vicar of Hursley. Second Edition. Post 8vo., cloth, 6s.

JOHN ARMSTRONG.

LIFE OF JOHN ARMSTRONG, D.D., late Lord Bishop of Grahamstown. By the Rev. T. T. CARTER, M.A., Rector of Clewer. With an Introduction by SAMUEL, LORD BISHOP OF OXFORD. Third Edition. Fcap. 8vo., with Portrait, cloth, 7s. 6d.

JOSHUA WATSON.

MEMOIR OF JOSHUA WATSON, Edited by EDWARD CHURTON, Archdeacon of Cleveland. New Edition. Crown 8vo., cloth, 7s. 6d.

BISHOP WILSON.

THE LIFE OF THE RIGHT REVEREND FATHER IN GOD, THOMAS WILSON, D.D., Lord Bishop of Sodor and Man. Compiled, chiefly from Original Documents, by the late Rev. JOHN KEBLE, M.A., Vicar of Hursley. In Two Parts, 8vo., cloth, 21s.

ANTONIO DE DOMINIS.

THE LIFE AND CONTEMPORANEOUS CHURCH HISTORY OF ANTONIO DE DOMINIS, Archbishop of Spalatro. By the late HENRY NEWLAND, D.D., Dean of Ferns. 8vo., cloth, 7s.

WALTER DE MERTON.

SKETCH OF THE LIFE OF WALTER DE MERTON, Lord High Chancellor of England, and Bishop of Rochester; Founder of Merton College. By EDMUND, Bishop of Nelson, New Zealand; late Fellow of Merton College. 8vo., 2s.

ARCHBISHOP HINCMAR.

THE LIFE AND TIMES OF HINCMAR, Archbishop of Rheims. By the late Rev. JAMES C. PRICHARD, M.A., Vicar of Mitcham. Fcap. 8vo., cloth, 5s.

CALIXTUS, ABBOT OF KONIGSLUTTER.

GERMAN THEOLOGY DURING THE THIRTY YEARS' WAR. THE LIFE and CORRESPONDENCE of GEORGE CALIXTUS, Lutheran Abbot of Königslutter, and Professor Primarius in the University of Helmstadt. By the Rev. W. C. DOWDING, M.A. Post 8vo., cloth, 8s. 6d.

FOOTPRINTS ON THE SANDS OF TIME. BIOGRAPHIES FOR YOUNG PEOPLE. Dedicated to her Nephews and Nieces by L. E. D. Fcap. 8vo., limp cloth, 2s. 6d.

THE LIFE OF AMBROSE BON- WICKE. 18mo., 1s.

THE LIFE OF GEORGE BULL, D.D., sometime Lord Bishop of St. David's. By ROBERT NELSON, Esq. 18mo., cloth, 1s. 6d.

THE SAINTLY LIFE OF MRS. MARGARET GODOLPHIN. 16mo. 1s.

Sacred Poetry.

THE AUTHORISED EDITIONS OF

THE CHRISTIAN YEAR,

With the Author's latest Corrections and Additions.

NOTICE.—Messrs. PARKER are the sole Publishers of the Editions of the "Christian Year" issued with the sanction and under the direction of the Author's representatives. All Editions without their imprint are unauthorized.

SMALL 4to. EDITION.			48mo. EDITION.		
	s.	d.		s.	d.
Handsomely printed on toned paper, with red border lines and initial letters. Cloth	10	6	Cloth, limp . . .	0	6
			Cloth boards . . .	0	9
FOOLSCAP 8vo. EDITION.			Roan	1	6
Cloth	3	6			
24mo. EDITION.			FACSIMILE OF THE FIRST EDITION, with a list of the variations from the Original Text which the Author made in later Editions. 2 vols., 12mo., boards		
Cloth	9	0			
32mo. EDITION.					
Cloth boards, gilt edges .	1	6			
Cloth, limp . .	1	0		7	6

The above Editions (except the Facsimile of the First Edition) are kept in a variety of bindings, which may be ordered through the Trade, or direct from the Publishers. The chief bindings are Morocco plain, Morocco Antique, Calf Antique, and Vellum, the prices varying according to the style.

KEBLE'S
COMPLETE POETICAL WORKS.
Uniform Edition. Fcap. 8vo., cloth.

THE CHRISTIAN YEAR. 3s. 6d.	PSALTER IN ENGLISH VERSE. 6s.
LYRA INNOCENTIUM. 6s.	MISCELLANEOUS POEMS. 6s.

By the Author of " The Christian Year."

LYRA INNOCENTIUM. Thoughts in Verse on Christian Children. Twelfth Edition, Fcap. 8vo. cloth, 6s.
48mo. edition, limp cloth, 6d.; cloth boards, 1s.

MISCELLANEOUS POEMS. By the Rev. JOHN KEBLE, M.A., Vicar of Hursley. [With Preface by G. M.] Third Edition. Fcap., cloth, 6s.

THE PSALTER, or, Psalms of David: In English Verse. Fourth Edition. Fcap. 8vo., cloth, 6s.
Cheap Edition.   18mo., cloth, 1s.
The above may also be had in various bindings.

OXFORD, AND 377, STRAND, LONDON.

A CONCORDANCE TO THE "CHRISTIAN YEAR." Fcap. 8vo., toned paper, cloth, 7s. 6d.

MUSINGS ON THE "CHRISTIAN YEAR." With GLEAN-INGS from Thirty Years' Intercourse with the late Rev. J. Keble, by CHARLOTTE M. YONGE; to which are added Recollections of Hursley, by FRANCES M. WILBRAHAM. Second Edition. Fcap. 8vo., cloth, 7s. 6d.

RE-ISSUE OF THE POETICAL WORKS

OF THE LATE

REV. ISAAC WILLIAMS.

THE CATHEDRAL; or, The Catholic and Apostolic Church in England. 32mo., cloth, 2s. 6d.

THE BAPTISTERY; or, The Way of Eternal Life. 32mo., cloth, 2s. 6d.

HYMNS FROM THE PARISIAN BREVIARY. 32mo., cloth, 2s. 6d. [*Nearly ready.*]

THE CHRISTIAN SCHOLAR. 32mo., cloth, 2s. 6d.

THOUGHTS IN PAST YEARS. 32mo., cloth, 2s. 6d.

The Fcap. 8vo. Editions of the following may also be obtained at the annexed prices.

THE CATHEDRAL. Fcap. 8vo., cloth, 5s.

THE BAPTISTERY. With Plates by Boetius & Bolswert. Fcap. 8vo., cloth, 7s. 6d.

THE CHRISTIAN SCHOLAR. Fcap. 8vo., cloth, 5s.

THOUGHTS IN PAST YEARS. Fcap. 8vo., cloth, 5s.

THE SEVEN DAYS OF THE OLD AND NEW CREATION. Fcap. 8vo., cloth, 3s. 6d.

OXFORD, AND 377, STRAND, LONDON.

SACRED POETRY (*continued*).

The Child's Christian Year.

Hymns for every Sunday and Holyday throughout the Year. Cheap Edition, 18mo., cloth, 1s.

Coxe's Christian Ballads.

CHRISTIAN BALLADS AND POEMS. By ARTHUR CLEVELAND COXE, D.D., Bishop of Western New York. A New Edition. Fcap. 8vo., cloth, 3s.

Also selected Poems in a packet, 32mo., 1s. *For Contents see page* 44.

Hymns on the Imitation of Christ.

THE INNER LIFE. HYMNS on the "Imitation of Christ" by THOMAS A'KEMPIS; designed especially for Use at Holy Communion. By the Author of "Thoughts from a Girl's Life," "Light at Eventide," &c. Fcap. 8vo., cloth, 3s.

Hymns on the Litany.

HYMNS ON THE LITANY. By A. C. Fcap. 8vo., on toned paper, cloth extra, 3s.

Morning Thoughts.

By a CLERGYMAN. Suggested by the Second Lessons for the Daily Morning Service throughout the year. 2 vols. Fcap. 8vo., cloth, 8s. each.

Poems

By the late Rev. SAMUEL RICKARDS, M.A., Rector of Stowlangtoft. Fcap. 8vo., toned paper, cloth, 3s. 6d.

The Cross, and Verses of Many Years.

By the Rev. CHARLES NEVILE, M.A., Prebendary of Lincoln, and Rector of Fledborough; and MARIA NEVILE. Fcap. 8vo., cloth, 7s. 6d.

Poems and Translations.

POEMS AND TRANSLATIONS. By E. H. HOUGHTON, M.A. Crown 8vo., limp cloth, 4s.

Florum Sacra.

SHORT POEMS by the Rev. J. M. SMYTTAN. 16mo., cloth. 1s.

Cornish Ballads.

THE CORNISH BALLADS AND OTHER POEMS of the Rev. R. S. HAWKER. Fcap. 8vo., cloth, 5s.

SACRED POETRY (continued).

The Bells of Botteville Tower;

A Christmas Story in Verse; and other Poems. By FREDERICK GEORGE LEE, Author of "The Martyrs of Vienne and Lyons," "Petronilla," "The King's Highway," &c. Fcap. 8vo., with Illustrations, cloth, 4s. 0d.

St. Chad's Day in Lichfield, A.D. 1643;

And other Short Poems. By the Rev. R. J. BUDDICOM, M.A., Vicar of Morton, Gainsborough. 24mo., limp cloth, 2s. 6d.

The Mother of Jesus,

AND OTHER POEMS. By ALAN BRODRICK, M.A., Ex. Coll. Oxon, Vicar of Whittlebury. Second Edition. Limp cloth, 3s.

Verses for the Blind and Afflicted.

18mo., in wrapper, 6d.

The Cleveland Psalter.

The Book of Psalms in English Verse. By E. CHURTON, M.A., Archdeacon of Cleveland. Fcap. 8vo., cloth, 7s. 6d.

Psalmody for the Christian Seasons.

Selected from the Cleveland Psalter. 18mo., limp cloth, 1s.

Hymns and Songs of the Church.

Translated and Composed by GEORGE WITHER. Edited by the Rev. HENRY E. HAVERGAL, M.A. 18mo., cloth, 3s.

Poems:

By LEWIS GIDLEY. Post 8vo., cloth, 3s.

Faith:

A Poem in Four Books. By LEWIS GIDLEY. Crown 8vo. cloth, 3s. 6d.

What is Truth?

A Poetical Dialogue on the Philosophy of Natural and Revealed Religion. By the Rev. WILLIAM VERNON HARCOURT, M.A. Crown 8vo., cloth, 2s. 6d.

In Memoriam.

In Memoriam J. C. P. Verses in Memory of the late Bishop PATTESON, by E. E. Large 8vo., cloth, 5s.

Hymnale

Secundum usum insignis ac Praeclarae Ecclesiae Sarisburiensis. 32mo., cloth, 3s. 6d.

Hymni Ecclesiae

E Breviariis quibusdam et Missalibus Gallicanis, Germanis, Hispanis, Lusitanis, descmptl. Collegit et Recensuit JOANNES M. NEALE, A.M., Collegii Sackvilliensis Custos. 18mo., cloth, 5s.

Devotional Works.

Meditations for the Forty Days of Lent.

By the Author of " Devotions before and after Holy Communion." With
a Prefatory Notice by the Archbishop of Dublin. 16mo., cloth, 3s. 6d.

Annus Domini.

A Prayer for each Day of the Year, founded on a Text of Holy Scripture.
By Christina G. Rossetti. 32mo., cloth, 3s. 6d.

Daily Steps towards Heaven.

A small pocket volume containing a few Practical Thoughts on the Gospel
History, with Text for Every Day in the Year, commencing with Advent.
Sixteenth Edition. Bound in roan, 2s. 6d. ; morocco, 5s.

Large Type Edition, square Crown 8vo., cloth, 3s.

The Every-day Companion.

By the Rev. W. H. Ridley, M.A., Rector of Hambleden, Bucks. Fcap. 8vo.,
cloth, 3s.

Prayers for Married Persons.

From Various Sources, chiefly from the Ancient Liturgies. Selected and
Edited by Charles Ward, M.A., Rector of Maulden. Second Edition.
Revised. 24mo., cloth, 4s. 6d.

Of the Imitation of Christ.

Four Books. By Thomas à Kempis. Small 4to., printed on thick toned paper,
with red border-lines, mediæval title-pages, ornamental initials, &c. Third
Thousand. Cloth, 12s.

Forms of Praise and Prayer.

In the Manner of Offices. For Private Use. Edited by the Hon. and Rev.
W. H. Lyttelton, M.A., Rector of Hagley. Crown 8vo., toned paper, limp
cloth, 3s. 6d. ; roan, 4s.

Evening Words.

Brief Meditations on the Introductory Portion of Our Lord's Last Discourse
with His Disciples. 18mo., cloth, price 3s.

The Cross of Christ;

Or, Meditations on the Death and Passion of Our Blessed Lord and Saviour.
Edited by Walter Farquhar Hook, D.D., F.R.S., Dean of Chichester.
Crown 8vo., cloth, 3s. 8d.

Preces Privatæ.

Reverendi Patris Lanceloti Andrewes Episc. Wintoniensis Preces Privatæ
Quotidianæ Græce et Latine. Fcap. 8vo., cloth, 4s.
Preces Privatæ in Studiosorum Gratiam Collectæ, et Regio Authoritate
Approbatæ; anno M D LXVIII. Londini Editæ ; ad Vetera Exemplaria Denuo
recognitæ. Square 16mo., cloth, 3s. 6d.

De Imitatione.

Thomæ à Kempis De Imitatione Christi. Libri Quatuor. 16mo., cloth, 3s. ;
Fcap. 8vo., cloth, 5s.

OXFORD, AND 377, STRAND, LONDON.

DEVOTIONAL WORKS (*continued*).

EDITED BY THE REV. E. B. PUSEY, D.D.

FRA THOME DE JESU.

THE SUFFERINGS OF JESUS. Composed by FRA THOMÉ DE JESU, of the Order of Hermits of St. Augustine, a Captive of Barbary. From the Portuguese. 2 vols., Fcap. 8vo., cloth, 7s.

SCUPOLI.

THE SPIRITUAL COMBAT, with the PATH of PARADISE; and the SUPPLEMENT; or, the Peace of the Soul. By SCUPOLI. (From the Italian.) 3s. 6d.
——————— Cheap Edition, in wrapper, 6d.
——————————— fine paper, limp cloth, 1s.

HORST.

PARADISE FOR THE CHRISTIAN SOUL. By HORST. Fourth Thousand. 2 vols., Fcap. 8vo., cloth, 6s. 6d.

From the "Paradise for the Christian Soul."

LITANIES. In the words of Holy Scripture. Royal 32mo., 6d.

AVRILLON.

THE YEAR OF AFFECTIONS; or, Sentiments on the Love of God, drawn from the Canticles, for every Day in the Year. By AVRILLON. Second Thousand. Fcap. 8vo., cloth, 6s. 6d.
A GUIDE FOR PASSING LENT HOLILY, in which is found for each day, Advice as to Practice, a Meditation, &c. By AVRILLON. From the French. Fourth Edition. Fcap. 8vo., cloth, 6s.
A GUIDE for PASSING ADVENT HOLILY. By AVRILLON. Translated from the French, and adapted to the use of the English Church. New Edition. Fcap. 8vo., cloth, 5s.

SURIN.

THE FOUNDATIONS OF THE SPIRITUAL LIFE. A Commentary on Thomas à Kempis. By SURIN. Fcap. 8vo., cloth, 4s. 6d.

NOUET.

THE LIFE OF JESUS CHRIST IN GLORY. Daily Meditations from Easter Day to the Wednesday after Trinity Sunday. By NOUET. Third Thousand. Fcap. 8vo., cloth, 6s.

ST. ANSELM.

MEDITATIONS AND SELECT PRAYERS OF ST. ANSELM. New Edition. Fcap. 8vo., cloth, 6s.

LENT READINGS FROM THE FATHERS. Fcap. 8vo., cloth, 5s.
ADVENT READINGS FROM THE FATHERS. New Edition. Fcap. 8vo., cloth, 3s. 6d.
In the Press, by the same Editor, in conjunction with the Lord Bishop of Brechin.
MANUAL FOR CONFESSORS, by M. l'Abbé GAUME. Translated from the French.

DEVOTIONAL WORKS (*continued*).

Private Devotion.

HELPS TO PRAYER AND DEVOTION: Intended chiefly for the Use of Young Persons who have been recently Confirmed. Crown 8vo, cloth, 8d.; Cheap Edition, 4d.

CULTUS ANIMÆ: Or, an Arraying of the Soul. Being Prayers and Meditations which may be used in Church. Fcap. 8vo., 2s. 6d.

A HELP TO PRAYER. In Six Tracts. By the Rev. W. Gresley, M.A., Prebendary of Lichfield. Fcap. 8vo., 1s.

DIVINE COUNSELS; Or, The Young Christian's Guide to Wisdom. Translated from Arvisenet. By William B. Caparn, M.A., Perpetual Curate of Drayton. 16mo., limp cloth, 1s.

THE PASTOR IN HIS CLOSET: Or, A Help to the Devotions of the Clergy. By John Armstrong, D.D., late Lord Bishop of Grahamstown. Third Edition. Fcap. 8vo., cloth, 2s.

THE THRESHOLD OF THE SANCTUARY. A Devotional Manual for Candidates for Holy Orders. By the Rev. E. D. Carr, M.A., Streatham. 18mo., cloth, 2s.

MARRIOTT'S PRAYERS FOR MORNING AND EVENING. Cloth, 1s. 6d.
PRAYERS FOR THE LITTLE ONES, by St C. F. 16mo., 3d.
MORNING AND EVENING PRAYERS AND HYMNS FOR ELDER AND YOUNGER CHILDREN. On a Card, 1d. each.
HARE'S HOLY MATRIMONY.—Devotional Exercises. 2d.
HENSLEY'S PRAYERS. 1d.

KEN'S (Bishop) MANUAL OF PRAYERS, adapted to general use. 6d.
HOURS OF PRAYER; being Devotions for the Third, Sixth, and Ninth Hours. With a Preface. Sixth Edition. Royal 32mo., vellum, 1s.
MANT'S DIAL OF PRAYER. 1s.
PSALM CXIX. IN PARTS FOR THE DAY. 16mo., 4d.
ON EARLY PRAYER. By Charles Page Eden, M.A. Cr. 8vo., 3d.

Family Prayers.

EARL NELSON'S FAMILY PRAYERS, with Responsions and Variations for the Different Seasons, for General Use. Sewed, 3d. each; with Psalter, cloth, 9d.
    The Calendar of Lessons; for Private or Family Use. Cloth, 6d.
    Family Prayers, with the Psalter and a Calendar of Lessons, for the Use of the Master. Cloth, 1s. Fourth revised Edition.

LITURGIA DOMESTICA: Services for every Morning and Evening in the Week; for the Use of Families. Third Edition, revised and enlarged. 18mo., cloth, 2s.

SHORT FORMS OF FAMILY PRAYER, by a Layman. Fcap. 8vo., cl., 2s. 6d.
BELLAIRS' PRAYERS FOR CHRISTIAN HOUSEHOLDS. New Edition. 1d.

BISHOP'S PRAYERS FOR THE USE OF FAMILIES. 18mo., 6d.
FAMILY PRAYERS, on large Card. 2d.

DEVOTIONAL WORKS (*continued*).

School and College Prayers.

BUTLER'S SCHOOL PRAYERS. With Music, 6d.

NORMAN'S MANUAL OF PRAYERS FOR THE USE OF SCHOOLS. 1s.

HEATHCOTE'S PRAYERS FOR SCHOOL-CHILDREN. 2d.

A DAILY TEXT-BOOK FOR THE USE OF SCHOOL-CHILDREN, &c., sewed, 6d.

BP. KEN'S MANUAL OF PRAYERS FOR WINCHESTER SCHOLARS. 18mo., 1s.

PRAYERS IN USE AT CUDDESDON COLLEGE. Fcap. 8vo., 1s.

Prayers for Divers Occasions.

AN ITINERARY, or Prayers for all that Travel. 6d.

DEVOTIONS FOR SEAFARING MEN. 6d.

PRAYERS FOR ARMY AND NAVY. 1d.

A LITANY OF OUR LORD'S WARNINGS. Suggestions for the Use of it, by KEBLE. 6d.

PRAYERS FOR PERSONS ASSOCIATED IN AID OF MISSIONS. 1d.

A Portuary.

A PORTUARY FOR THE LAITY. Long Primer, 24mo., limp cloth, 2s. 6d.; limp morocco, gilt edges, 5s.

The same, 32mo., limp cloth, 6d.; cloth, 9d.; morocco, 1s. 6d.
—— thick paper, morocco, 2s.; best circuit morocco. 3s. 6d.
—— 48mo., red rubrics, limp russia, 2s. 6d.

The same, With Hymns Ancient and Modern and Introits, 32mo., limp cloth, 1s.
—— 24mo., cloth, 3s.; morocco, 6s.

In Sickness and Affliction.

THOUGHTS DURING SICKNESS. By ROBERT BRETT, Author of "The Doctrine of the Cross," &c. Fourth Edition, Fcap. 8vo., limp cloth, 1s. 6d.

BREVIATES FROM HOLY SCRIPTURE. Arranged for use by the Bed of Sickness. By the Rev. G. ARDEN, M.A. Second Edition. Fcap., cloth, 2s.

LE MESURIER'S PRAYERS FOR THE SICK. 3s.

THE ORDER FOR THE VISITATION OF THE SICK. Fcap. 8vo., sd., 1d.

DEVOTIONS FOR THE SICK. From the Tracts for Parochial Use. Fcap., cloth, 2s. 6d.

The Clewer Manuals.

THE CLEWER MANUALS. Edited by the Rev. T. T. CARTER, M.A., Rector of Clewer.

PART I. Daily Offices of Prayer and other Devotions. 18mo., 1s.

PART II. Hours of Prayer, Litanies, &c. 18mo., limp cloth, 1s.

PART III. Instructions and Devotions for Adult Baptism and Con-

firmation. 18mo., limp cloth, 1s.

PART IV. Repentance. 18mo., limp cloth, 1s. 6d.

PART V. No. 1. Instructions on the Holy Eucharist. 18mo., sewed, 1s.

DEVOTIONAL WORKS *(continued)*.

For the Lord's Supper.

DEVOTIONS BEFORE AND AFTER HOLY COMMUNION.
With Prefatory Note by KEBLE. Fifth Edition, in red and black, on toned paper, 32mo., cloth, 2s.

The above, with the Service, cloth, 2s. 6d.

THE OLD WEEK'S PREPARATION TOWARDS A WORTHY RECEIVING OF THE HOLY SACRAMENT OF THE LORD'S SUPPER. Edited by WILLIAM FRASER, B.C.L., Curate of Alton. Feap. 8vo., cloth, 2s.

A SHORT AND PLAIN INSTRUCTION FOR THE BETTER UNDERSTANDING OF THE LORD'S SUPPER. By Bp. WILSON. 32mo., with red rubrics, cloth, gilt edges, 2s.

—— A Cheap Edition, sewed, 6d.; limp cloth, 8d.

OFFICIUM EUCHARISTICUM. A Preparatory Service to a Devout and Worthy Reception of the Lord's Supper. By EDWARD LAKE, D.D. 32mo., cloth, 1s. 6d.

THE LORD'S SUPPER. From the Parochial Tracts. 18mo., limp cl., 1s.

EUCHARISTICA: Meditations and Prayers on the Most Holy Eucharist, from old English Divines. With an Introduction by the late Bishop WILBERFORCE. 32mo., cl., 2s. 6d.

—— A Cheap Edition, 32mo., limp cloth, 1s.

DEVOTIONS FOR HOLY COMMUNION, from Horst's "Paradise for the Christian Soul." 18mo., limp cl., 1s.

SPIRITUAL COMMUNION. Devotions from the Works of Bps. PATRICK and WILSON. 32mo., 6d.

The Practical Christian's Library.

A Series of Selections from the Writings of the most eminent Divines of the Church of England.

DEVOTIONAL SERIES.

Uniform, in 18mo., limp blue cloth, price 1s. each.

1. A KEMPIS Imitation of Christ, 1s.
2. ANDREWES' (Bp.) Devotions, 1s.
3. AUGUSTINE's Confessions, 1s.
4. COSIN's (Bp.) Devotions, &c., 1s.
5. KEN's Manual of Prayers, with Catechism and Directions, 1s.
6. SHERLOCK's Self-Examination and Holy Communion, 1s.
7. SHERLOCK's Meditations and Prayers, 1s.
8. SPINCKES' Devotions, 1s.
9. SUTTON's Disce Vivere, 1s.
10. —— Disce Mori, 1s.
11. TAYLOR's (Bp.) Holy Living, 1s.
12. —— Holy Dying, 1s.
13. —— Golden Grove, with Selection of Offices and Prayers, 1s.
14. WILSON's Lord's Supper, 1s.
15. —— Sacra Privata, 1s.
16. —— Maxims of Piety and Morality, 1s.

DEVOTIONAL WORKS (*continued*).

Oxford Editions of Devotional Works.

Fcap. 8vo., chiefly printed in Red and Black, on Toned Paper.

Andrewes' Devotions.

DEVOTIONS. By the Right Rev. LAUNCELOT ANDREWES. Translated from the Greek and Latin, and arranged anew. Cloth, 5s.

The Imitation of Christ.

FOUR BOOKS. By THOMAS A KEMPIS. A new Edition, revised. Cloth, 4s.

Laud's Devotions.

THE PRIVATE DEVOTIONS of Dr. WILLIAM LAUD, Archbishop of Canterbury, and Martyr. Antique cloth, 5s.

Spinckes' Devotions.

TRUE CHURCH OF ENGLAND MAN'S COMPANION IN THE CLOSET. By NATHANIEL SPINCKES. Florized borders, antique cloth, 4s.

Sutton's Meditations.

GODLY MEDITATIONS UPON THE MOST HOLY SACRA-MENT OF THE LORD'S SUP-PER. By CHRISTOPHER SUTTON, D.D., late Prebend of Westminster. A new Edition. Antique cloth, 5s.

Taylor's Golden Grove.

THE GOLDEN GROVE: A Choice Manual, containing what is to be Believed, Practised, and Desired or Prayed for. By Bishop JEREMY TAYLOR. Antique cloth, 3s. 6d.

Taylor's Holy Living.

THE RULE AND EXERCISES OF HOLY LIVING. By Bishop JEREMY TAYLOR. Antique cloth, 4s.

Taylor's Holy Dying.

THE RULE AND EXERCISES OF HOLY DYING. By Bishop JEREMY TAYLOR. Antique cloth, 4s.

Wilson's Sacra Privata.

THE PRIVATE MEDITATIONS, DEVOTIONS, and PRAYERS of the Right Rev. T. WILSON, D.D., Lord Bishop of Sodor and Man. Now first printed entire. Cloth, 4s.

Devout Communicant.

THE DEVOUT COMMUNICANT, exemplified in his Behaviour before, at, and after the Sacrament of the Lord's Supper: Practically suited to all the Parts of that Solemn Ordinance. Seventh Edition, revised. Edited by Rev. G. MOUL-TRIE. Antique cloth, 4s.

ΕΙΚΩΝ ΒΑΣΙΛΙΚΗ.

THE PORTRAITURE OF HIS SACRED MAJESTY KING CHARLES I. in his Solitudes and Sufferings. Cloth, 5s.

Ancient Collects.

ANCIENT COLLECTS AND OTHER PRAYERS, Selected for Devotional Use from various Rituals, with an Appendix on the Collects in the Prayer-book. By WILLIAM BRIGHT, D.D. Fourth Edition. Antique cloth, 5s.

The Christian Seasons.

TEACHINGS FROM THE CHURCH'S YEAR. Post 8vo., cloth, 6s.

See also Commentary on the Epistles and Gospels from the Fathers, p. 11, and Pusey's Advent and Lent Readings, Avrillon, &c., p. 31.

Tracts.

TRACTS FOR THE CHRISTIAN SEASONS. First Series. Edited by JOHN ARMSTRONG, D.D., late Lord Bishop of Grahamstown. 4 vols. complete, Fcap. 8vo., cloth, price 12s.

TRACTS FOR THE CHRISTIAN SEASONS. Second Series. Edited by JOHN ARMSTRONG, D.D., late Lord Bishop of Grahamstown. 4 vols. complete, Fcap. 8vo., cloth, price 10s.

TRACTS FOR THE CHRISTIAN SEASONS. Third Series. Edited by JAMES RUSSELL WOODFORD, D.D., Lord Bishop of Ely. 4 vols., Fcap. 8vo., cloth, price 14s.

Sermons.

SERMONS FOR THE CHRISTIAN SEASONS. First Series. Edited by JOHN ARMSTRONG, D.D., late Lord Bishop of Grahamstown. 4 vols., Fcap. 8vo., cloth, price 16s.

SERMONS FOR THE CHRISTIAN SEASONS. Second Series. Edited by the Rev. JOHN BARROW, D.D., late Principal of St. Edmund Hall, Oxford. 4 vols., Fcap. 8vo., cloth, 16s.

SHORT SERMONS FOR FAMILY READING, following the Course of the Christian Seasons. By the Rev. J. W. BURGON, M.A., Vicar of St. Mary-the-Virgin's, Oxford. First Series. 2 vols., Fcap. 8vo., cloth, 8s.

————————————— Second Series. 2 vols., Fcap. 8vo., cl., 8s.

Miscellanea.

SIX LECTURES ON THE EVENTS OF HOLY WEEK. By WILLIAM MATURIN, B.A., Perpetual Curate of Grangegorman, Dublin. Crown 8vo., cloth, 2s. 6d.

THE MAN OF SORROWS. The Mental Suffering of our Lord and Saviour Jesus Christ during His Passion. By the Ven. WALTER B. MANT, M.A., Archdeacon of Down. Fcap. 8vo., cloth, 2s. 6d.

A SIMPLE CATECHISM ON THE SEASONS OF THE CHURCH, explained by the History of the New Testament. For the use of Children in Schools. In wrapper, price 3d., or 2s. 6d. per dozen.

CATECHETICAL NOTES on THE SAINTS' DAYS. 1s.

HYMNS FOR THE WEEK AND SEASONS. 12mo., cloth, 4s.

THE CLOSING DAYS OF OUR LORD'S MINISTRY on EARTH. Fcap. 8vo., 2d.

GOOD-FRIDAY, Harmonized from the Four Gospels. 32mo., 3d.

OXFORD, AND 377, STRAND, LONDON.

Crown 8vo., in roan binding, 12s.; calf limp, or calf antique, 16s.;
best morocco, or morocco limp, 18s.

The Service-Book of the Church of England,

BEING A NEW EDITION OF "THE DAILY SERVICES OF THE UNITED CHURCH OF ENGLAND AND IRELAND,"

ARRANGED ACCORDING TO THE NEW TABLE OF LESSONS.

In 1849, the revival of Daily Service in many of our parish
churches suggested the publication of a volume containing those
portions of the Bible which were appointed for the First and
Second Lessons printed together with so much of the Prayer-
book as was required in the Daily Service of the Church.

In 1858, a new edition being required, several improvements were
adopted, and references given, by which the Daily Lessons were
rendered available for use in reading the Sunday Lessons also.

The new "Prayer-book (Table of Lessons) Act, 1871," has
necessitated reprinting nearly the whole book, and opportunity
has been taken of still further adding to the improvements.

The Lessons appointed for the Immoveable Festivals are printed
entire in the course of the Daily Lessons where they occur. For the
Sundays and Moveable Festivals, and for the days dependent on
them, a table containing fuller references, with the initial words
and ample directions where the Lesson may be found, is given.
Where the Lesson for the Moveable Feast is not included entire
amongst the Daily Lessons, it is printed in full in its proper place.
Also in the part containing Daily Lessons, greater facilities have
been provided for verifying the references.

There are also many modifications in the arrangement, wherein
this Service-book differs from the Prayer-book: the Order for the
Administration of the Holy Communion is printed as a distinct
service, with the Collects, Epistles, and Gospels, which belong to
the same: the Psalms immediately follow Daily Morning and
Evening Prayer: the Morning and Evening Lessons also are by
this arrangement brought nearer to the Service to which they
belong, while the Occasional Offices are transferred to the end of
the book. This plan of arrangement will shew the aim and object
of the work, viz. to provide a convenient and portable volume for
those persons who have the privilege of attending the appointed
Daily Service in the Church or read it in their own houses.

Church Psalmody.

The Psalter.

THE PSALTER, or Canticles and Psalms of David, Pointed for Chanting, upon a new principle; with Explanations and Directions. By the late STEPHEN ELVEY, Mus. Doc. Eighth Edition. 8vo., cloth, 6s.
———— Ninth Edition. Fcap. 8vo., limp cloth, 2s. 6d.
———— THE CANTICLES separately. Fcap. 8vo., in wrapper, 6d.

THE OXFORD AND CAMBRIDGE PSALTER, with the Canticles and Athanasian Creed, Pointed and Punctuated for Chanting. Edited by the Rev. ARTHUR BEARD, M.A., and the Rev. F. HENRY GRAY, M.A. Third Edition. 8vo., cloth, 3s. 6d.
———— 18mo., limp cloth, 1s.; cloth bound, 1s. 6d.
———— THE CANTICLES separately, 8vo., in cloth wrapper, 6d.
———— 18mo., sewed, 1d.; in cloth wrapper, 2d.

THE PSALTER, with the Gregorian Tones adapted to the several Psalms; as also the Canticles in the Prayer-book, and the Creed of St. Athanasius. Second Edition. 18mo., cloth, 3s.
———— THE CANTICLES separately, in wrapper, 3d.

THE PSALTER, Pointed, by OUSELEY and MONK. 4to. Edition, with Chants in Short Score, 4s.
———— 12mo. Edition, Vocal Parts. Each 1s. 6d.
———— 18mo. Edition. Words only, 9d.
———— —————— with Proper Psalms, 1s.

Anthems.

A COLLECTION OF ANTHEMS USED IN THE CATHEDRAL AND COLLEGIATE CHURCHES OF ENGLAND AND IRELAND. By WILLIAM MARSHALL, Mus. Doc. Sixth Edition. Post 8vo., cloth, 3s.

Hymns.

THE ANGLICAN HYMN-BOOK. Edited by the Rev. ROBERT CORBET SINGLETON, M.A., and EDWIN GEORGE MONK, Mus. Doc. Words and Music. short score, 4to., cloth, 6s.
———— Words and Music, short score, 18mo., cloth, 2s. 6d.
———— Words and Treble part, square 16mo., cloth, 1s. 6d.
———— Words only, 16mo., cloth, 1s.; 32mo., 6d.

THE ENGLISH HYMNAL. A Hymn-Book for the Use of the Church of England. 18mo., cloth, 1s.

HYMNS SELECTED FROM THE CHURCH HYMN AND TUNE BOOK. 16mo., cloth, 1s.

THE PAROCHIAL HYMN-BOOK, for the Use of the Church of England. Selected and Arranged by the Rev. J. ROBINSON, M.A. Fcap. 8vo., cloth, 1s. 10d.

PSALMS AND HYMNS FOR PAROCHIAL USE. 12mo., roan, 1s. 6d.

Parochial.

Parish Work.

THE CHURCH AND THE SCHOOL; or, Hints on Clerical
Life. By HENRY WALFORD BELLAIRS, M.A., late one of Her Majesty's
Inspectors of Schools. Crown 8vo., cloth, 2s. 6d.

SHORT NOTES OF SEVEN YEARS' WORK IN A
COUNTRY PARISH. By R. F. WILSON, M.A., Vicar of Rownhams,
Prebendary of Sarum, and Examining Chaplain to the Bishop of Salisbury.
Fcap. 8vo., cloth, 4s.

THE CHURCH'S WORK IN OUR LARGE TOWNS. By
GEORGE HUNTINGTON, M.A., Rector of Tenby, and Domestic Chaplain of
the Rt. Hon. the Earl of Crawford and Balcarres. Second Edition, revised
and enlarged. Crown 8vo., cloth, 6s.

Parochial Papers.

Edited by the Rev. J. ARMITSTEAD, M.A.

No.	s.	d.	No.	s.	d.
1. Parish Choirs.			7. Secular Subjects	. 1	0
2. School	. 1	0	8. Fabric of the Church	. 1	0
3. Missions	. 1	0	9. Parochial Charities .	. 1	0
4. Parochial Visiting—Rich	. 1	0	10. The Congregation	. 1	0
5. School, No. 2	. 1	0	11. Baptism	. 1	0
6. Parochial Visiting—Poor	. 1	0	12. Confirmation	. 1	0

On Pastoral Visitation.

A MANUAL OF PASTORAL VISITATION, intended for
the Use of the Clergy in their Visitation of the Sick and Afflicted. By
a PARISH PRIEST. Dedicated, by permission, to His Grace the Archbishop
of Dublin. Second Edition. Crown 8vo., limp cloth, 3s. 6d.; roan, 4s.

THE CURE OF SOULS. By the Rev. G. ARDEN, M.A.,
Rector of Winterborne-Came, and Author of "Breviates from Holy Scripture," &c. Fcap. 8vo., cloth, 2s. 6d.

Miscellanea.

STRONG CALICO LENDING WRAPPERS
for the Parochial Tracts, with tapes,
&c. 1d. each.

DR. ACLAND'S FORMS FOR REGISTER-
ING THE SANITARY CONDITION OF
VILLAGES. 8vo. 50 in wrapper,
1s. 6d.

—— PRECAUTIONS AGAINST CHO-
LERA. 50 for 1s.

—— HEALTH, WORK, AND PLAY.
6d.

A PARTING GIFT FOR YOUNG WOMEN
LEAVING SCHOOL FOR SERVICE. 4d.

THE PREVAILING SIN OF COUNTRY
PARISHES. ½d. each.

NO NEARER TO HEAVEN. 1d.

TOTAL ABSTINENCE NOT CHRISTIAN
TEMPERANCE. By the Rev. E. S.
LOWNDES, M.A. Crown 8vo., 1s. 6d.

HARVEST HYMN, WITH MUSIC. 4to.,
4d. Words only, 8vo., 1d.

HINTS FOR HARVEST SERVICES. By
the Rev. J. BAINES, Little Marlow.
Crown 8vo., 1s.

PARKER'S CHURCH CALENDAR AND
GENERAL ALMANAC. Issued An-
nually. Crown 8vo., 6d.

PAROCHIAL (*continued*).

Catechising.

THE CATECHIST'S MANUAL; with an Introduction by the late SAMUEL WILBERFORCE, D.D., Lord Bishop of Winchester. Fifth Thousand. Crown 8vo., limp cloth, 6s.

CATECHETICAL LESSONS. Designed to aid the Clergy in Public Catechising. FIRST SERIES. Fcap. 8vo.

1. The Apostles' Creed. 6d.	8. The Morning and Evening Prayer, and the Litany. 1s.
2. The Lord's Prayer. 6d.	9. The Miracles of our Lord. Pt. I. 1s.
3. The Ten Commandments. 6d.	10. The Miracles of our Lord. Pt. II. 1s.
4. The Two Sacraments. 6d.	
5. The Parables. Part I. 1s.	11. On the Saints' Days. 1s.
6. The Parables. Part II. 1s.	12. On Miscellaneous Subjects. 1s. 6d.
7. The Thirty-nine Articles. 1s. 6d.	

The above Set complete in 2 vols., cloth, price 10s.

SECOND SERIES. Catechetical Lessons on the Book of Common Prayer. By the Rev. Dr. FRANCIS HESSEY.

13. Introduction, &c. 6d.	16—21. Collects, Epistles, and Gospels, &c. Price 6d. each Part.
14. Morning and Evening Prayer. 1s.	22. Saints' Days, Title-page, Preface, &c. 1s.
15. Litany, &c. 6d.	

The above Set in one vol., cloth, price 6s.

THE CHURCH CATECHISM EXPLAINED, with a view to the Correction of Error in Religion and Viciousness of Life. By the Rev. EDWARD CRAZER, M.A., Incumbent of Little Drayton, Salop. Fcap. 8vo., cloth, 2s. 6d.

QUESTIONS ON THE COLLECTS, EPISTLES, and GOSPELS throughout the Year. Edited by the Rev. T. L. CLAUGHTON. Part I. Fourth Edition, cloth, 2s. 6d.

—— Part II. Fourth Edition. Cloth, 2s. 6d.

NICHOLSON'S EXPOSITION OF THE CATECHISM OF THE CHURCH OF ENGLAND. A New Edit. 1s. 6d.

PROGRESSIVE EXERCISES ON THE CHURCH CATECHISM. By the Rev. HENRY HOPWOOD, M.A.
Parts 1, 2, and 3. Analytical Exercises. 2d. each.
Part 4. Biblical Exercises. 3d.
AN OUTLINE OF THE CHURCH CATECHISM. Royal 8vo. In a Tabular form. 1s.

SHERLOCK'S PARAPHRASE OF THE CHURCH CATECHISM. 18mo., 6d.

HINSLEY'S STEPS TO UNDERSTANDING THE CHURCH CATECHISM. 1d.

WEBNHAM'S QUESTIONS ON THE COLLECTS. 1s.

QUESTIONS ON THE TABERNACLE AND ITS SERVICES. 18mo., 1s. 6d.

BEAVEN'S CATECHISM ON THE ARTICLES. 1s. 6d.

On Baptism.

THE GIFT OF THE HOLY GHOST IN BAPTISM AND CONFIRMATION. 32mo., 3d.

HOLY BAPTISM. An Earnest Appeal to the Unbaptised. Sewed, 1d.

A SHORT CATECHISM ON THE BAPTISMAL VOW AND CONFIRMATION. Edited by the Ven. H. P. FFOULKES, Archdeacon of Montgomery. Fcap. 8vo., 2d.

VAUGHAN'S DOCTRINE OF BAPTISM, &c. 1s.

AN INTRODUCTION TO THE CHURCH CATECHISM, for the Use of those who have not been Baptized. 1d.

CARDS FOR SPONSORS. 6d. per doz.

BAPTISMAL HYMN, with Tune. 4to., 4d.

See also the Parochial Tracts, p. 46.

PAROCHIAL (*continued*).

On Confirmation.

THE CONFIRMATION CLASS-BOOK ; Notes for Lessons, with
Appendix, containing Questions and Summaries for the Use of the Candidates. By R. M. Holmes, LL.B., Rector of March Gibbon, Bucks; Diocesan Inspector of Schools; Author of the "Catechist's Manual." Fcap. 8vo.,
limp cloth, 2s. 6d.

Also, in wrapper, The Questions and Summaries separate, 4 sets of
128 pp. in packet, 1s. each.

THE ORDER OF CONFIRMATION illustrated by Select
Passages from Old English Divines; With Lessons, &c. By the Rev.
Henry Hopwood, M.A. Third Edition, 32mo., cloth, 2s. 6d.

PREPARATION FOR CONFIRMATION. By the Rev. Richard
Lowndes, M.A., Vicar of Sturminster Newton. 16mo., cloth, 1s. 6d.

CONFIRMATION ACCORDING TO SCRIP-
TURE. 3d.

NOTES ON CONFIRMATION. By a
Priest. Sewed, 6d.

SHORT CATECHISM ON BAPTISMAL
VOW AND CONFIRMATION. 2d.

QUESTIONS BEFORE CONFIRMATION,
50 for 1s.

ARDEN'S LECTURES ON CONFIRMA-
TION. 1s.

KARSLAKE'S MANUAL FOR THOSE
ABOUT TO BE CONFIRMED. Crown
8vo., 1s.

A MANUAL FOR CHRISTIANS, FOR
THE AFTER CONFIRMATION. By
Edward Hawkins, D.D. Fcap.
8vo., 6d.

See also The Parochial Tracts on Confirmation, p. 48.

On the Lord's Supper.

WHAT IS UNWORTHY RECEIVING?
1 Cor. xi. 29. 1d.

CLAUGHTON'S DUTY OF PREPARING
FOR THE LORD'S SUPPER. 1d.

*See also Parochial Tracts, p. 48, Catechetical Lessons, p. 40, and
for Devotional Works, p. 35.*

On the Prayer-book.

A COMPANION TO THE PRAYER-BOOK,
compiled from the best sources,
18mo., cloth, 1s.

ARCHBISHOP LAUD ON LITURGY,
EPISCOPACY, AND CHURCH RITUAL.
16mo., 2s.

SALKELD'S GODLY SINCERITY OF
THE COMMON PRAYER-BOOK VIN-
DICATED. 6d.

FREEMAN'S PLAIN DIRECTIONS FOR
UNDERSTANDING SERVICES. 3d.

TEN REASONS WHY I LOVE MY
PRAYER-BOOK. 12 for 3d.

On Public Worship.

CAPARN'S MEDITATIONS IN CHURCH
BEFORE DIVINE SERVICE. 32mo.,
sewed, 6d.

REVERENCE IN CHURCH. A Card, 3d.

REASONS FOR STAYING AWAY FROM
CHURCH. Reprinted from the
"Penny Post." 8vo. 3d. per dozen.

*See also Parochial Tracts on Church and Church Service, p. 47,
and Parochial Papers, p. 59.*

HISTORICAL TALES,

Illustrating the Chief Events in Ecclesiastical History, British and Foreign,
adapted for General Reading, Parochial Libraries, &c.

*Fcap. 8vo., neatly done up in cloth, with a Frontispiece.
Price One Shilling each.*

ENGLAND. Vol. I.

		s.	d.
1. The Cave in the Hills; or, Cæcilius Viriathus	.	1	0
6. Wild Scenes amongst the Celts	.	1	0
7. The Rivals; a Tale of the Anglo-Saxon Church	.	1	0
10. The Black Danes	.	1	0
14. The Alleluia Battle; or, Pelagianism in Britain	.	1	0

The above Tales in one vol., cloth, price 5s.

ENGLAND. Vol. II.

		s.	d.
16. Alice of Fobbing	.	1	0
18. Aubrey de L'Orne; or, The Times of S. Anselm	.	1	0
21. The Forsaken; or, The Times of N. Dunstan	.	1	0
24. Walter the Armourer; or, The Interdict	.	1	0
27. Agnes Martin; or, The Fall of Wolsey	.	1	0

The above Tales in one vol., cloth, price 5s.

AMERICA AND OUR COLONIES.

		s.	d.
3. The Chief's Daughter	.	1	0
5. The Convert of Massachusetts	.	1	0
20. Wollingham	.	1	0
23. The Catechumens of the Coromandel Coast	.	1	0
28. Rose and Minnie; or, The Loyalists	.	1	0

The above Tales in one vol., cloth, price 5s.

FRANCE AND SPAIN.

		s.	d.
2. The Exiles of the Cebenna	.	1	0
22. The Dove of Tabenna; and The Revenue	.	1	0
25. Larache; a Tale of the Portuguese Church	.	1	0
29. Dores de Gualdim; a Tale of the Portuguese Revolution of 1640	.	1	0

The above Tales in one vol., cloth, price 5s.

EASTERN AND NORTHERN EUROPE.

		s.	d.
8. The Lazar House of Leros	.	1	0
11. The Conversion of S. Vladimir	.	1	0
13. The Cross in Sweden	.	1	0
17. The Northern Light	.	1	0
26. The Daughters of Pola	.	1	0

The above Tales in one vol., cloth, price 5s.

ASIA AND AFRICA.

		s.	d.
4. The Lily of Tiflis	.	1	0
9. The Quay of the Dioscuri; a Tale of Nicene Times	.	1	0
12. The Sea Tigers; a Tale of Mediæval Nestorianism	.	1	0
15. The Bride of Ramcuttah	.	1	0
19. Lucia's Marriage	.	1	0

The above Tales in one vol., cloth, price 5s.

OXFORD, AND 377, STRAND, LONDON.

TALES, ALLEGORIES, &c.

Suitable for Presents and Reward Books, from 4d. to 5s.

	s.	d.
Seléne; or, The Queen of the Fairy Cross. 16mo. .	0	4
Old Christmas. 16mo.	0	6
Mount Gars; or, Marie's Christmas-Eve. 16mo. .	0	6
Rhymes and Pictures from Pocci. 16mo. . . .	0	6
Little Footprints on the Old Church Path. 16mo., cloth .	0	8
Florum Sacra. 16mo., cloth	1	0
Flowers from the Garden of the Church	1	0
The Matin Bell. 16mo.	1	0
Henry Vernon; or, The Little Anglo-Indian . . .	1	0
The Garden of Life; an Allegory. 16mo. . . .	1	0
Ann Ash. Fcap. 8vo.	1	0
The Messages of the Prince	1	6
The Pastor of Wellbourn. 16mo., cloth . . .	2	0
The Messages of the Prince. Fcap. 8vo., cloth . .	2	6
Ada's Thoughts; or, The Poetry of Youth. Fcap. 8vo. .	2	6
The History of our Lord, in Easy Verse. Small 4to., cloth	2	6
The Two Homes, by the Author of "Amy Grant" . .	2	6
The Singers of the Sanctuary. 16mo., cloth . . .	2	6
First Voyage of Rodolph the Voyager, by Sewell. 12mo., cl.	2	6
Second Voyage of Rodolph the Voyager. 12mo., cloth .	2	6
The Pilgrim's Progress, for the use of Members of the Church of England. *Illustrated.* 8vo., cloth . .	3	6
———— A Cheaper Edition. Crown 8vo., cloth .	2	6
Speculation: a Tale. Fcap. 8vo., cloth	2	6
The Californian Crusoe. A Mormon Tale. Fcap., cloth .	2	6
The Scholar and the Trooper. Fcap. 8vo. . .	2	6
Alice Lisle: A Tale of Puritan Times. Fcap. 8vo. . .	2	6
For Life; a Story in Two Parts. By Louis Sand. Cr. 8vo., cl.	3	0
Chronicles of Camber Castle. Cloth	3	0
Short Readings for Sunday Scholars. Fcap. 8vo., cloth .	3	6
The Orphans, a Tale, by E. C. Phillips. Cr. 8vo., cl. gilt	3	6
Some Years After. Fcap. 8vo.	5	0
Kenneth; or, The Rear-Guard of the Grand Army . .	5	0
Atheline; or, The Castle by the Sea. 2 vols. . . .	5	0
Mignonette: A Sketch. 2 vols.	5	0
Hawkstone, a Tale, by Sewell. 2 vols. Fcap. 8vo., cloth	5	0

TALES FOR YOUNG MEN AND WOMEN.

In Fcap. 8vo., neatly done up in cloth, with a Frontispiece.

	s. d.		s. d.		s. d.
Mother and Son .	1 0	Servants' Influence	0 6	The Two Cottages	1 0
The Recruit .	1 0	Railway Accident	1 0	Squitch . .	1 0
The Strike . .	1 0	Wanted, a Wife .	1 0	The Politician .	1 0
James Bright, the		Irrevocable . .	1 0	Two to One .	1 0
Shopman .	1 0	The Tenants at		Hobson's Choice .	0 6
Jonas Clint . .	1 0	Tinkers' End .	1 0	Susan . . .	0 4
The Sisters . .	1 0	Windyside Hall .	1 0	Mary Thomas ;	
Caroline Elton ;		False Honour .	1 0	or, Disarm at	
or, Vanity and		Old Jarvis's Will	1 0	Evenly . .	0 4
Jealousy . .	0 6				

TALES AND ALLEGORIES.

Reprinted from the "PENNY POST."

Fcap. 8vo., in wrapper, Illustrated.

	s. d.		s. d.		s. d.
The Child of the		Mary Wilbram .	0 4	Little Foibles .	0 7
Temple . .	1 0	Marion . .	0 4	Marthunus . .	0 4
The Heart-stone .	0 10	Mary Merton .	0 2	Fanny Dale .	1 6
Fairton Village .	0 8	The Two Widows	0 3	Gill's Lap . .	0 8
Footprints in the		Left Behind .	0 2	Old Winterton's	
Wilderness	0 6	Little Tales .	0 4	Will . . .	0 4
Tales of an Old		Little Allegories,		Annerton the For-	
Church . .	0 4	containing the		getful . .	0 2
Margaret of Coo-		Sunday Morn-		Eustathes the Con-	
way . .	0 4	ing's Dream, &c.	0 7	stant . .	0 2

COXE'S CHRISTIAN BALLADS.

Dreamland. 1d.	Chimes of England. 1d.	St. Silvan's Bell. 1d.
Hymn of Boyhood. 1d.	Churchyards. 1d.	Daily Services. 1d.
England. 1d.	Little Woodmere. 1d.	The Calendar, and "I
Lenten Season. 1d.	Matin Bells and Curfew.	love the Church." 1d.
Chronicles. 1d.	1d.	

The Set in a Packet, 32mo., 1s.

SEVEN FAIRY TALES, Illustrated.

16mo., in wrapper.

Little Ino C. and his	Ulric and Laura. 4d.	Samuesl and his Sister
Companions. 4d.	Rose and the Fairy Help-	Soignense. 4d.
Sholto and his Little Dog	ful. 4d.	Bommatura. 4d.
Bousvaky. 4d.	The Fairy Devairgille. 4d.	

The above Tales in one vol., cloth, price 2s. 6d.

COTTAGE PICTURES FROM THE OLD TESTAMENT.

A Series of Twenty-eight large folio Engravings, brilliantly coloured by hand. The Set, 7s. 6d.

COTTAGE PICTURES FROM THE NEW TESTAMENT.

A Series of Twenty-eight large folio Engravings, brilliantly coloured. The Set, 7s. 6d.

N.B. Upwards of Eight Thousand Sets of these Cottage Pictures have already been sold. They are recommended by the National Society, in whose "Monthly Paper" appeared a series of lessons on Holy Scripture especially adapted to this series of Prints.

SCRIPTURE PRINTS FOR PAROCHIAL USE.

PRINTED IN SEPIA, WITH ORNAMENTAL BORDERS.

Price One Penny each; or the set in ornamental envelope, One Shilling.

1. The Nativity.
2. St. John's Preaching.
3. The Baptism of Christ.
4. Jacob's Dream.
5. The Transfiguration.
6. The Good Shepherd.
7. The Tribute Money.
8. The Preparation for the Cross.
9. The Crucifixion.
10. Leading to Crucifixion.
11. Healing the Sick.
12. The Return of the Prodigal.

The above are also kept mounted and varnished, 3d. each.

THE PENNY POST.

A CHURCH OF ENGLAND ILLUSTRATED MAGAZINE, issued Monthly. Price One Penny.

Each number consists of Thirty-two Pages 8vo, printed on toned paper, with several Illustrations, and contains—ARTICLES on Practical Religious Duties; on Doctrinal Questions; on the Work of the Church at Home and Abroad; and on Topics of the Day which call for the attention of Churchmen. EXTRACTS FROM OLD AUTHORS, enforcing the truths of Christianity, and explaining the doctrines of the Church. These are selected from the Early Fathers, the Old English Divines, or other Standard Writers. TALES, of Country and Home Life; Shorter Tales; Parish Incidents, &c.; Historical Tales, &c. SHORT TALES and ALLEGORIES, suitable for Children. SHORT ESSAYS and Descriptive Pieces, of a practical and religious tendency. ARCHAEOLOGICAL, GEOGRAPHICAL, or SCIENTIFIC Articles, with Illustrations, and written in a plain and familiar style, will from time to time be introduced. THE EDITOR'S BOX, for asking and answering questions relating especially to Church matters, will be continued as formerly.

Monthly—One Penny.

Subscribers' Names received by all Booksellers and Newsmen.

* *Arrangements can be made, by application to the Publishers, for LOCALIZING this Magazine.*

THE PENNY POST, in volumes.

Vol. I. 1851, to Vol. IV. 1854, 18mo, cloth, 1s. 6d. each.
Vol. V. 1855, to Vol. XXIII. 1873, 8vo, sewed, 1s.; cloth, 1s. 6d. each.

TRACTS FOR PAROCHIAL USE.

No. of Tract	THE CHIEF TRUTHS.	A Shilling Packet contains
198.	The Holy Trinity	25
163.	The Incarnation	25
194.	The Passion	25
43.	The Resurrection	25
64.	The Ascension	25
65.	The Judgment	25
217.	The Holy Ghost	10
216.	The Holy Catholic Church and Communion of Saints	10
210.	The Forgiveness of sins	20
200.	The Life Everlasting	10
164.	A Scripture Catechism on the Church	4d. each.
166.	A Catechism concerning the Church	9

One of each of the above 12 Tracts in a Blue Packet, 1s.

THE CREEDS, &c.

The Creed.

1.	Exposition of Apostles' Creed	9
198.	Questions and Answers on Athanasian Creed	16
134.	Letter on Athanasian Creed	9

The Lord's Prayer.

| 178. | The Lord's Prayer | 30 |
| 134. | Scripture Paraphrase on the Lord's Prayer | 30 |

The Commandments.

209.	I. Thou shalt have none other Gods but Me	30
210.	II. Thou shalt not make to thyself any graven image	40
211.	III. Thou shalt not take the name of the Lord thy God in vain. Swear not at all	40
13 L.		40
6.	IV. How to spend the Lord's Day. Where were you last Sunday?	10
198.		30
212.	V. Honour thy Father and Mother	40
166.	VI. Thou shalt do no Murder	30
213.	VII. Thou shalt not commit adultery	40
62.	The Unmarried Wife	10
214.	VIII. Thou shalt not steal	40
215.	IX. Thou shalt not bear false witness	40
76.	Truth and Falsehood	10
216.	X. Thou shalt not covet	40

One of each of the above 16 Tracts in a Blue Packet, 1s6d.

No. of Tract	BAPTISM.	A Shilling Packet contains
208.	Baptismal Service explained	9
167.	Holy Baptism	9
199.	Friendly Words on Baptism	13
171.	Questions about Baptism answered out of Scripture	13
54.	Registration and Baptism	10
141.	Why three are God-Parents	25
199.	Choice of God-Parents	50
162.	Advice to God-Parents	25
109.	Who should be Sponsors	10

One of each of the above 8 Tracts in a Blue Packet, 1s.

THE LORD'S SUPPER.

120.	The Lord's Supper	9
70.	Plain Speaking to Non-Communicants	10
132.	One Word more on the Lord's Supper	20
17.	The Lord's Supper the Christian's Privilege	25
140.	Have you neared to Communion?	10
192.	Am I fit to receive the Lord's Supper?	25
166.	Have you Communicated since Confirmation?	10
168.	A Persuasive to frequent Communion	10
201.	Devotions Preparatory to Lord's Supper	20

One of each of the above 9 Tracts in a Blue Packet, 2d.

CONFIRMATION.

169.	Confirmation Service explained	13
20.	Questions for Confirmation	13
47.	—— 2nd Series	17
98.	Preparation for Confirmation	20
149.	Words before Confirmation	20
91.	Hints for Day of Confirmation	30
196.	Catechism on Confirmation	10
87.	Words after Confirmation	10

One of each of the above 8 Tracts in a Blue Packet, 2d.

OFFICES, &c.

172.	Marriage Service explained	9
114.	Are you going to be married?	25
113.	Duties of the Married State	25
206.	Service for Visitation of Sick	9
162.	The Churching Service explained	13
2.	Words after Churching	10
64.	The Communion Service	10

No. of Tract.		A Shilling Packet contains	No. of Tract.		A Shilling Packet contains
121.	The Burial Service explained	9	41.	Devotions for Women Labouring with Child	10
48.	Thoughts about Burials	10	42.	Devotions during time of Cholera	25
	One of each of the above 9 Tracts in a Blue Packet, 1d.			*One of each of the above 11 Tracts in a Blue Packet, 10d.*	
	HOLY DAYS AND SEASONS.			**FOR THE SICK AND AFFLICTED.**	
21.	How to spend Advent	60	73.	Hints for the Sick. Part I.	12
23.	How to keep Christmas	20	110.	—— Parts II. and III.	12
93.	New Year's Eve	10	81.	Friendly Advice to the Sick	9
22.	How to keep Lent	10	95.	Scripture Readings during Sickness	12
55.	Ken's Advice during Lent	20	112.	Are you better for your Sickness?	25
129.	Trust for Holy Week	9	94.	Will you give Thanks for your Recovery?	20
108.	Trust for Good Friday	12	197.	Form of Thanks for Recovery	20
103.	How to keep Easter	25	64.	Devotions for the Desolate	10
60.	Neglect of Ascension Day	20	173.	Devotions for Widows	20
176.	How to keep Whitsuntide	50	70.	Comfort for the Blind	10
	One of each of the above 10 Tracts in a Blue Packet, 6d.		134.	Patience in Affliction	16
			16.	To Mourners	12
	THE CHURCH, AND CHURCH SERVICE.			*One of each of the above 12 Tracts in a Blue Packet, 9d.*	
12.	Be in time for Church	25		**FOR PENITENTS.**	
16.	"No Things to go in"	25	157.	Devotions for Penitents	12
207.	The Gate of the Lord's House	9	101.	Comfort to the Penitent	25
108.	What do we go to Church for?	12	127.	Tracts for Female Penitents. Pt. I.	25
39.	How to behave in Church	12	124.	—— Part II.	10
191.	Conduct in Church	10	139.	—— Part III.	9
47.	On making Responses in Church	12	191.	—— Part IV.	9
42.	Do you Sing in Church?	25	198.	—— Part V.	9
145.	Daily Common Prayer	10	200.	—— Part VI.	12
3.	Do you ever Pray?	40	200.	—— Part VII.	12
61.	No Kneeling, no Praying	10		*One of each of the above 9 Tracts in a Blue Packet, 9d.*	
127.	Word to the Deaf about Church	50			
71.	Church or Market	25		**PRAYERS, HYMNS, &c.**	
63.	Beauty of Churches	20	142.	Morning and Evening Family Prayers	10
152.	Doors or Open Seats	12	176.	Daily Office for Families, 6d. each.	
47.	Plain Hints to Bell-Ringers	25	0.	Morning and Evening Prayers for Young Persons	60
112.	Church Choirs	25	7.	Morning, Evening, and Midnight Hymns	25
139.	Plain Hints to a Parish Clerk	25	141.	Morning and Evening Hymns for Young Persons	20
131.	Plain Hints to Sextons	20	90.	Prayers for Schoolmasters and Schoolmistresses	64
172.	Plain Hints to an Overseer	20	204.	Prayers for those who work hard	20
190.	Plain Hints to a Churchwarden	16	159.	Seven Meditations	20
	One of each of the above 21 Tracts in a Blue Packet, 1s.		164.	Meditation on Day of Judgment	50
			111.	Litany for Ember Weeks	10
	DEVOTIONS FOR THE SICK.		73.	On Family Prayer	50
32.	Prayer for Patients	12	165.	On Private Prayer	25
35.	Litanies for the Sick	12	202.	On Common Prayer	50
34.	Self-Examination	12	37.	Meditation	12
83.	Confession	34		*One of each of the above 14 Tracts in a Blue Packet, 7d.*	
86.	Prayers for various occasions	12			
37.	Prayers during long Sickness	12			
93.	Devotions for Friends of the Sick	10			
89.	Devotions when there appeareth but small hope of recovery	25			
68.	Thanksgiving on abatement of Pain	12			

No. of Tract		A Shilling Packet contains	No. of Tract		A Shilling Packet contains
	ADVICE AND EXHOR-TATION.		119.	Flee for thy Life	25
140.	Word to the Parents of my Flock	12	49.	Be sure your Sin will find you out	25
62.	Exhortation to Young Women	12	110.	The Tongue	10
169.	Exhortation to Repentance	25	121.	Make your Will before you are Ill	20
88.	Advice to Young Servant	10	84.	Think before you Drink	25
97.	To Masters of Families	25	185.	Why will ye die?	50
149.	Word to the Aged	25		*One of each of the above 14 Tracts in a Blue Packet, 7d.*	
194.	Examine Yourselves	10			
157.	Few Words on Christian Unity	12		**MISCELLANEOUS.**	
96.	To Sunday School Teachers	12	6.	The Bootlevies	10
61.	To Parents of Sunday Scholars	25	146.	Twelve Rules to live by Grace	50
117.	Word to the Pauper	25	104.	The Christian's Cross	25
92.	Farewell Words to an Emigrant	25	152.	Consult your Pastor	25
63.	Few Words to Travellers	50	117.	Reverence	25
154.	The Farmer's Friend	10	56.	Schism	10
78.	Few Words to Farmers 2d. each.		169.	Conversion	12
	One of each of the above 15 Tracts in a Blue Packet, 10d.		4.	Almsgiving every man's Duty	15
	WARNING & CAUTION.		66.	Weekly Almsgiving	10
194.	Thou God seest me	25	122.	Honesty	9
69.	Word of Warning to the Sinner	25	17.	Sailor's Voyage	10
93.	Word of Caution to Young Men	12	162.	Evil Angels	10
122.	Now is the Accepted Time	50	106.	The Holy Angels	10
15.	Sudden Death	50	192.	Fasting	10
144.	Never mind; we are all going to the same place	25	201.	Pray for your Pastor	25
176.	"Too late"	12	197.	Are all Apostles?	25
67.	Shut out	25	74.	Right way of reading Scripture	10
			147.	Love your Prayer-book	25
				One of each of the above 18 Tracts in a Blue Packet, 1s.	

The Set of the above 15 Blue Packets, containing 180 Tracts, 10s. 6d.

TALES AND ALLEGORIES. Illustrated. 2d. EACH.

Originally published in the "Parochial Tracts."

* Alice Grant.
Bye and Bye.
* Complaints and their Cure.
* The Cloud upon the Mountain. 3d.
* The Curate's Daughter.
* The Day that never came.
Edward Ellard; or, Who's afraid?
* Edwin Forth; or, The Emigrant.

* The Fair on Whit-Monday.
* Hannah Dean.
* Harry Fulton.
The Hop-Picker.
* It might have been Worse.
Her Son has gone down while it was yet Day.
Joseph and his Brethren.
Jane Smith's Marriage.
Little Geoffrey.
* Mary Faber.

The Modern Martyr.
* Mr. Sharpley.
* Nothing Lost in the Telling.
* The Prodigal.
The Promised Estate.
Richard Revesley's Legacy.
* The Rock and the Sand.
* "That shalt not steal;" or, The School Feast.
* Tony Dilke.
Too Old to be Questioned.

N.B. Those marked with an asterisk are bound up in a volume, entitled "Tales and Allegories," cloth, 2s. 6d. The remainder in "Parochial Tales," price 2s. 6d.

COTTAGERS' SERIES. Illustrated. 2d. EACH.

Originally published in the "Parochial Tracts."

The Cottage Pig-Stye.
Keeping Poultry no Loss.
Mrs. Martin's Bee-hive.
The Honest Widow.

The Village Shop.
Who Pays the Funerals?
Mrs. Morton's Walk.

Two-pence for the Clothing Club.
The Widower.

The Set bound in cloth, price 2s.

The Set of 169 Tracts and 37 Tales, &c., to be had complete in Seven Volumes, cloth, price 31s.

ARCHITECTURAL WORKS.

Glossary of Architecture.

A CONCISE GLOSSARY OF TERMS USED IN GRECIAN, ROMAN, ITALIAN, AND GOTHIC ARCHITECTURE. By JOHN HENRY PARKER, C.B., M.A., F.S.A. A New Edition, revised. Fcap. 8vo., with 470 Illustrations, in ornamental cloth, 7s. 6d.

The large Edition, in Medium 8vo., with Plates, will shortly be reprinted.

Alterthumliches Wortregister, a German Index to the Glossary. 8vo., 2s. 6d.

Vocabulaire Archeologique, a French Index to the Glossary. 8vo., 2s. 6d.

Architectural Manual.

AN INTRODUCTION to the STUDY OF GOTHIC ARCHITECTURE. By JOHN HENRY PARKER, C.B., M.A., F.S.A. Fourth Edition, Revised and Enlarged, with 100 Illustrations, with a Topographical and a Glossarial Index. Fcap. 8vo., in ornamental cloth, 5s.

Mediæval Domestic Architecture.

SOME ACCOUNT OF DOMESTIC ARCHITECTURE IN ENGLAND, from Richard II. to Henry VIII. (or the Perpendicular Style). With numerous Illustrations of Existing Remains from Original Drawings. By the EDITOR OF "THE GLOSSARY OF ARCHITECTURE." In 2 vols., 8vo., £1 10s.

Also,

FROM EDWARD I. TO RICHARD II. (the Edwardian Period, or the Decorated Style). 8vo., cloth, 21s.

Gothic Architecture.

AN ATTEMPT TO DISCRIMINATE THE STYLES OF ARCHITECTURE IN ENGLAND, from the Conquest to the Reformation: with a Sketch of the Grecian and Roman Orders. By the late THOMAS RICKMAN, F.S.A. Medium 8vo. *A new Edition in preparation.*

Mediæval Castles.

THE MILITARY ARCHITECTURE OF THE MIDDLE AGES. Translated from the French of M. VIOLLET-LE-DUC, by M. MACDERMOTT, Esq., Architect. With 151 original French Engravings. Medium 8vo., cloth, 21s.

Roman Archæology.

THE ARCHÆOLOGY OF ROME. By JOHN HENRY PARKER, C.B., M.A., F.S.A. Medium 8vo. Illustrated by Plans, Diagrams, &c. Vol. I., in 2 Parts, 8vo., cloth, price £1 1s.

ARCHÆOLOGICAL WORKS.

The Calendar of the Prayer-book.

THE CALENDAR OF THE PRAYER-BOOK ILLUSTRATED. (Comprising the first portion of the "Calendar of the Anglican Church," illustrated, enlarged, and corrected.) With upwards of Two Hundred Engravings from Mediæval Works of Art. Fcap. 8vo., Sixth Thousand, ornamental cloth, 6s.

Mediæval Church Furniture.

INVENTORY OF FURNITURE AND ORNAMENTS RE-MAINING IN ALL THE PARISH CHURCHES OF HERT-FORDSHIRE, in the last year of the Reign of King Edward the Sixth: Transcribed from the Original Records, by JOHN EDWIN CUSSANS, F.R.Hist.S. Crown 8vo., limp cloth, 4s.

Archæological Handbook.

THE ARCHÆOLOGIST'S HANDBOOK. By HENRY GODWIN, F.S.A.—A summary of the materials for the investigation of the Monuments of this country, arranged chiefly under periods, from the earliest times to the fifteenth century,—together with Tables of Dates, Kings, &c., Lists of Coins, Cathedrals, Castles, Monasteries, &c. Crown 8vo., cloth, 7s. 6d.

Mediæval Glass Painting.

AN INQUIRY INTO THE DIFFERENCE OF STYLE OB-SERVABLE IN ANCIENT GLASS PAINTINGS, especially in England, with Hints on Glass Painting, by the late CHARLES WINSTON. With Corrections and Additions by the Author. A New Edition. 2 vols., Medium 8vo., with numerous coloured Engravings, cloth, £1 11s. 6d.

INTRODUCTION TO THE STUDY OF GLASS PAINTING. By the late CHARLES WINSTON. 8vo., 2s. 6d.

Mediæval Brasses.

A MANUAL OF MONUMENTAL BRASSES. Comprising an Introduction to the Study of these Memorials, and a List of those remaining in the British Isles. With Two Hundred Illustrations. By the late Rev. HERBERT HAINES, M.A., of Exeter College, Oxford. 2 vols., 8vo., 12s.

Mediæval Armour.

ANCIENT ARMOUR AND WEAPONS IN EUROPE. By JOHN HEWITT, Member of the Archæological Institute of Great Britain. The work complete, from the Iron Period of the Northern Nations to the Seventeenth Century. 3 vols., 8vo., £2 10s.

Mediæval Ironwork.

SERRUBERIE DU MOYEN-AGE. Par RAYMOND BORDEAUX. Forty Lithographic Plates, by G. Bouet, and numerous Woodcuts. Small 4to., cloth, 20s.

Mediæval Sketch-book.

FACSIMILE OF THE SKETCH-BOOK OF WILARS DE HONECORT, AN ARCHITECT OF THE THIRTEENTH CENTURY. With Commentaries and Descriptions by M.M. LASSUS and QUICHERAT. Translated and Edited by the Rev. ROBERT WILLIS, M.A., F.R.S. With 64 Facsimiles, &c. Royal 4to., cloth, £3 10s. *The English letterpress separate, for the purchasers of the French edition,* 4to., 15s.

ARCHÆOLOGICAL WORKS (*continued*).

Mediæval Manners, &c.
OUR ENGLISH HOME: Its Early History and Progress. With Notes on the Introduction of Domestic Inventions. Third Edition. Crown 8vo., 5s.

Sepulchral Crosses.
A MANUAL for the STUDY of SEPULCHRAL SLABS and CROSSES of the MIDDLE AGES. By the Rev. Edward L. Cutts, B.A. 8vo., illustrated by upwards of 300 Engravings. 6s.

Domesday Book.
DOMESDAY BOOK, or the Great Survey of England of William the Conqueror, A.D. MLXXXVI. Facsimile of the part relating to Oxfordshire. Folio, cloth, price 8s.

A Translation, with Notes, &c., in preparation.

Northern Antiquities.
THE PRIMEVAL ANTIQUITIES of ENGLAND and DEN-MARK COMPARED. By J. J. A. Worsaae. Translated and applied to the Illustration of similar remains in England, by W. J. Thoms, F.S.A., &c. With numerous Illustrations. 8vo., cloth, 5s.

Anglo-Saxon Antiquities.
THE FAIRFORD GRAVES. A Record of Researches in an Anglo-Saxon Burial-place in Gloucestershire. By William Michael Wylie, B.A., Fellow of the Society of Antiquaries of London. 4to., 10s. 6d.

Early British Archæology.
OUR BRITISH ANCESTORS: WHO AND WHAT WERE THEY? An Inquiry serving to elucidate the Traditional History of the Early Britons by means of recent Excavations, Etymology, Remnants of Religious Worship, Inscriptions, &c. By the Rev. Samuel Lysons, M.A., F.S.A., Rector of Rodmarton. Post 8vo., cloth, 12s.

Serials.
THE "ARCHÆOLOGIA." Volumes issued occasionally under the direction of the Society of Antiquaries.
THE ARCHÆOLOGICAL JOURNAL. Published under the Direction of the Central Committee of the Archæological Institute of Great Britain and Ireland, for the Encouragement and Prosecution of Researches into the Arts and Monuments of the Early and Middle Ages. 5 vols. With numerous Illustrations. 8vo., cloth, £5. *A few complete sets only remaining; separate parts, price 2s. each.*
THE GENTLEMAN'S MAGAZINE from 1856 to 1865, (Vol. I. to Vol. XIX.,) containing Articles on Archæology, History, Architecture, &c.—Unpublished Documents.—Proceedings of Antiquarian Societies, &c. 8vo., 16s. per volume. *Separate numbers, price 2s. each.*
ARCHÆOLOGIA CAMBRENSIS, the Journal of the Cambrian Archæological Association. Fourth Series. Vol. I., II., III., and IV. 8vo., cloth, each £1 10s.

TOPOGRAPHICAL WORKS.

English Counties.
OR, AN ARCHITECTURAL ACCOUNT OF EVERY CHURCH IN

BEDFORDSHIRE, 2s. 6d.	CAMBRIDGESHIRE, 4s.
BERKSHIRE, 2s. 6d.	HUNTINGDONSHIRE, 2s. 6d.
BUCKINGHAMSHIRE, 2s. 6d.	OXFORDSHIRE, 2s. 6d.

SUFFOLK, *with Engravings*, 7s. 6d.

Its Dedication.—Supposed date of Erection or Alteration.—Objects of Interest in or near.—Notices of Fonts.—Glass, Furniture,—and other details.—Also Lists of Dated Examples, Works relating to the County, &c.

N.B. Each Church has been personally surveyed for the occasion by some competent antiquary.

Westminster Abbey.

GLEANINGS FROM WESTMINSTER ABBEY. By GEORGE GILBERT SCOTT, R.A., F.S.A. With Appendices supplying Further Particulars, and completing the History of the Abbey Buildings, by Several Writers. Second Edition, enlarged, containing many new Illustrations by O. Jewitt and others. Medium 8vo., cloth, gilt top, 15s.

Oxfordshire.

A HANDBOOK FOR VISITORS TO OXFORD. Illustrated by One Hundred and Twenty-eight Woodcuts by Jewitt, and Twenty-nine Steel Plates by Le Keux. *A New Edition in the Press.*

THE RAILWAY TRAVELLER'S WALK THROUGH OXFORD. A New Edition with Fifty-two Illustrations. 18mo., in ornamental wrapper, 1s.

GUIDE TO ARCHITECTURAL ANTIQUITIES in the Neighbourhood of Oxford. 8vo., cloth, 12s.

MEMOIRS ILLUSTRATIVE OF THE HISTORY AND ANTIQUITIES OF THE COUNTY AND CITY OF OXFORD, communicated to the Archæological Institute, June, 1850. 8vo., cloth, with Illustrations, 10s. 6d.

SOME REMARKS UPON THE CHURCH OF GREAT HASELEY, OXFORDSHIRE, together with Extracts from Delafield's MS. in the Bodleian Library, entitled "Notitia Haslejana." Second Edition, 8vo., cloth, 5s.

SOME ACCOUNT OF THE ABBEY CHURCH OF ST. PETER AND ST. PAUL, AT DORCHESTER, OXFORDSHIRE. By the Rev. HENRY ADDINGTON, B.A., with Notes, &c., by the Rev. W. C. MACFARLANE, Incumbent of Dorchester. 8vo., cloth, 6s.

THE EARLY HISTORY OF WOODSTOCK MANOR and its Environs; With later Notices: by EDWARD MARSHALL, M.A., formerly Fellow of C.C.C., Oxford; Diocesan Inspector of Schools for the Deanery of Woodstock. Post 8vo., cloth, price 12s.

AN ACCOUNT of the PARISH OF SANDFORD, in the Deanery of Woodstock, Oxon. *By the same Author.* Crown 8vo., cloth, 3s.

AN ACCOUNT of the TOWNSHIP OF CHURCH ENSTONE, Oxon. *By the same Author.* Crown 8vo., cloth, 3s.

A HISTORY OF THE TOWNSHIP OF IFFLEY, Oxfordshire. A New Edition. *By the same Author.* Crown 8vo., cloth, 4s.

OXFORD, AND 377, STRAND, LONDON.

TOPOGRAPHICAL WORKS (*continued*):

ABINGDON—An Account of the Brotherhood of the Holy Cross, and of the Hospital of Christ in Abingdon, by FRANCIS LITTLE, 1627. Edited by C. D. COBHAM, B.C.L. Fcap. 8vo., cloth, 4s.

CANTERBURY—The Architectural History of the Cathedral. By Professor WILLIS, M.A., F.R.S., &c. With Woodcuts and Plans. 8vo., cloth, 10s. 6d.

CHESTER, The Mediæval Architecture of. By JOHN HENRY PARKER, M.A., F.S.A. With an Historical Introduction by the Rev. FRANCIS GROSVENOR. Illustrated by Engravings. 8vo., cloth, 6s.

DOVER—The Church and Fortress of Dover Castle. By the Rev. JOHN PUCKLE, M.A., Vicar of St. Mary's, Dover; Rural Dean. With Illustrations from the Author's Drawings. Medium 8vo., cloth, 7s. 6d.

DURHAM, Illustrations of the Mediæval Antiquities of the County of. By J. TAVENOR PERRY and CHARLES HEXMAN, Jun., Architects. Super-royal Folio, in wrapper, £1 11s. 6d.

NORTHAMPTON, Architectural Notices of the Churches in the Archdeaconry of. With Illustrations. Royal 8vo., cloth, £1 1s.

NORWICH, Proceedings of the Archæological Institute at, 1847. 8vo., 10s. 6d.

PORTSMOUTH—The Story of the "Domus Dei" of Portsmouth, commonly called the Royal Garrison Church. By H. P. WRIGHT, M.A., Chaplain to the Forces, &c. Crown 8vo., 7s. 6d.

SCOTLAND—Descriptive Notices of some of the Ancient Parochial and Collegiate Churches of Scotland, with Woodcuts by O. Jewitt. 8vo., 5s.

WALTHAM—The Tract "De Inventione Sanctæ Crucis nostræ in Monte Acuto et de Ductione Ejusdem apud Waltham," from the MS. in the British Museum, with Introduction and Notes by WILLIAM STUBBS, M.A., Regius Professor of Modern History. Royal 8vo., 5s.; Demy 8vo., 3s. 6d.

WELLS, The Architectural Antiquities of the City of. By JOHN HENRY PARKER, C.B., M.A., F.S.A. Illustrated by Plans and Views. Medium 8vo., cloth, 5s.

—— Iconography of the West Front of Wells Cathedral, with an Appendix on the Sculptures of other Mediæval Churches in Oxford. By CHARLES ROBERT COCKERELL, R.A. With Plates, 4to., cloth, 10s. 6d.

WINCHESTER, Proceedings of the Archæological Institute at, 1845. 8vo., 10s. 6d.

WORCESTER—On the Ancient British Antiquities and Folk-lore of Worcestershire. By J. ALLIES. 8vo., cloth, 15s.

YORK, Memoirs Illustrative of the History and Antiquities of the County and City of, communicated to the Archæological Institute of Great Britain and Ireland, 1846. With 134 Illustrations. 8vo., cloth, 10s. 6d.

—— The Architectural History of the Cathedral. By Professor WILLIS, M.A., F.R.S., &c. With Woodcuts and Plans. 8vo., 2s. 6d.

54 JAMES PARKER AND CO.

PRACTICAL WORKS.

Gothic Ornament.
A SERIES OF MANUALS OF GOTHIC ORNAMENT.
No. 1. Stone Carving. 16mo., 1s. No. 2. Mouldings. 16mo., 1s. No. 3. Surface Ornament. 16mo., 1s.

Art.
ART APPLIED TO INDUSTRY: A Series of Lectures by William Burges, F.R.I.B.A. Medium 8vo., cloth, 4s.

English Country Houses.
FORTY-FIVE VIEWS AND PLANS of recently-erected Mansions, Private Residences, Parsonage-Houses, Farm-Houses, Lodges, and Cottages; with the actual cost of each, and A PRACTICAL TREATISE ON HOUSE-BUILDING. By William Wilkinson, Architect, Oxford. Royal 4to., ornamental cloth, £1 16s.

Ancient Church-Plate, &c.
SPECIMENS OF ANCIENT CHURCH-PLATE, SEPULCHRAL CROSSES, &c. 4to., cloth, 10s.

Painted Glass.
A PLEA FOR PAINTED GLASS, by F. W. Oliphant. Fcap. 8vo., sewed, 1s. 6d.

Restoration.
A PLEA FOR THE RESTORATION OF CHURCHES, by Sir G. G. Scott. 8vo., 3s. 6d.

WORKING DRAWINGS OF CHURCHES,
WITH VIEWS, ELEVATIONS, SECTIONS, AND DETAILS.

Warmington Church. Royal folio, cloth, 10s. 6d. A fine thirteenth-century Church. About 115 ft. by 47.

St. Leonard's, Kirkstead. Small folio, 5s. A small Church in the Early English style. 42 ft. by 19.

Minster Lovell Church. Folio, 5s. A very elegant specimen of the Perpendicular style. To hold 350 persons.

Littlemore Church. Second Edition. Folio, 5s. A small modern Church, in the Early English style. Size, 68 ft. by 55, and 40 ft. high. Cost, £800. Holds 210 persons.

Shottesbrooke Church. Folio, 3s. 6d. A good and pure specimen of the Decorated style.

Wilcote Church. Folio, 3s. 6d. A small Church in the Decorated style. Size, 60 ft. by 30. Estimated cost, £364. Holds 160 persons.

St. Bartholomew's Chapel, Oxford. Folio, 3s. 6d. A small Chapel in the Early Perpendicular style. Size, 24 ft. by 16. Estimated cost, £236. Holds 90 persons.

Stanton Church. Folio, 5s. A small Church in the Early English style. Calculated for 200 persons; Cost about £800.

Oxford Burial-ground Chapel. Folio, 10s. 6d. 1, Norman. 2, Early English. 3, Decorated. Separately, each 5s.

PUBLISHED BY THE OXFORD ARCHITECTURAL SOCIETY.
Sixpence per Sheet.

Open Seats—2. Hanwell.
3. Steeple Aston.
4. Stanton Harcourt; Exham.
5. Littlemore.

Bench Ends—6. Steeple Aston. Sheet 1.
7. Ditto. Sheet 2.

Oak Stalls—8. Beauchamp Chapel.
9. Tatland, Beverley, &c.

Fonts—10. Heckington,(Decorated).
11. Newenden, (Norman).

Reredos—12. St. Michael's, Oxford.
Pulpits—15. Wolvercot, (Perpen.).
16. Beaulieu, (Decorated).
17. St. Giles', Oxford, (Dec.); with Coombs, (Perpen.).
Screens—19. Dorchester and Stanton Harcourt.
Stone Desk—20. Crowle Church, (Norman).
Lich-Gates—21—23. Rockenham, West Wickham, Pulborough, Boughton Monchelsea.

OXFORD, AND 377, STRAND, LONDON.

THE OXFORD POCKET CLASSICS.

A SERIES OF GREEK AND LATIN CLASSICS FOR THE USE OF SCHOOLS.

GREEK POETS.

	Cloth.			Cloth.
	s. d.			*s. d.*
Æschylus	3 0	Sophocles	3 0
Aristophanes. 2 vols. .	6 0	Homeri Ilias . . .	3 6
Euripides. 3 vols. . .	6 6	—— Odyssea . . .	3 0
—— Tragœdiæ Sex	3 6		

GREEK PROSE WRITERS.

	Cloth.			Cloth.
Aristotelis Ethica . .	2 0	Thucydides. 2 vols. . .	5 0
Demosthenes de Corona, et Æschines in Ctesiphontem	2 0	Xenophontis Memorabilia .	1 4
		—— Anabasis . .	2 0
Herodotus. 2 vols. . .	6 0		

LATIN POETS.

	Cloth.			Cloth.
Horatius	2 0	Lucretius	2 0
Juvenalis et Persius . .	1 6	Phædrus	1 4
Lucanus	2 6	Virgilius . ; . .	2 6

LATIN PROSE WRITERS.

	Cloth.			Cloth.
Cæsaris Commentarii, cum Supplementis Auli Hirtii et aliorum	2 6	Ciceronis Tusc. Disp. Lib. V.	2 0
—— Commentarii de Bello Gallico	1 6	Ciceronis Orationes Selectæ .	3 6
		Cornelius Nepos . . .	1 4
Cicero De Officiis, de Senectute, et de Amicitia . . .	2 0	Livius. 4 vols.	6 0
		Sallustius	2 0
		Tacitus. 2 vols. . . .	5 0

The above volumes may also be had sewed in wrapper, at about Sixpence per volume less than cloth.

OXFORD, AND 377, STRAND, LONDON.

TEXTS WITH SHORT NOTES.

UNIFORM WITH THE SERIES OF "OXFORD POCKET CLASSICS."

GREEK WRITERS.

SOPHOCLES.

	s. d.		s. d.
Ajax (*Text and Notes*) .	1 0	Antigone (*Text and Notes*) .	1 0
Electra " .	1 0	Philoctetes " . . .	1 0
Œdipus Rex " . .	1 0	Trachiniæ " . . .	1 0
Œdipus Coloneus " .	1 0		

The Notes only, in one vol., cloth, 5s.

ÆSCHYLUS.

	s. d.		s. d.
Persæ (*Text and Notes*) .	1 0	Choephoræ (*Text and Notes*) .	1 0
Prometheus Vinctus " .	1 0	Eumenides " .	1 0
Septem Contra Thebas " .	1 0	Supplices " .	1 0
Agamemnon " .	1 0		

The Notes only, in one vol., cloth, 5s. 6d.

ARISTOPHANES.

The Knights (*Text and Notes*)	1 0	Acharnians (*Text and Notes*)	1 0
The Birds (*Text and Notes*) .	1 6		

EURIPIDES.

	s. d.		s. d.
Hecuba (*Text and Notes*) .	1 0	Phœnissæ (*Text and Notes*) .	1 0
Medea " . . .	1 0	Alcestis . " .	1 0
Orestes " . .	1 0	The above, Notes only, in one vol., cloth, 5s.	
Hippolytus " . .	1 0	Bacchæ " .	1 0

DEMOSTHENES.

De Corona (*Text and Notes*) .	3 0	Olynthiac Orations . .	1 0

HOMERUS.		XENOPHON.	
Ilias, Lib. i.—vi. (*Text and Notes*)	2 0	Memorabilia (*Text and Notes*)	2 6
ÆSCHINES.		**ARISTOTLE.**	
In Ctesiphontem (*Text and Notes*) . . .	2 0	De Arte Poetica (*Text and Notes*). [*In preparation.*]	

OXFORD, AND 377, STRAND, LONDON.

TEXTS WITH SHORT NOTES (*continued*).

LATIN WRITERS.

VIRGILIUS.

		s. d.			*s. d.*
Bucolica (*Text and Notes*)	.	1 0	Æneidos, Lib. i.—iii. (*Text*		
Georgica	"	. 1 0	*and Notes*) . . .	.	1 0

HORATIUS.

Carmina, &c. (*Text and Notes*)	2 0	Epistolæ et Ars Poetica (*Text*		
Satiræ	"	. 1 0	*and Notes*) . .	. 1 0

The Notes only, in one vol., cloth, 2s.

SALLUSTIUS.

Jugurtha (*Text and Notes*)	. 1 6	Catilina (*Text and Notes*)	. 1 0

M. T. CICERO.

In Q. Cæcilium — Divinatio		In Catilinam	1 0
(*Text and Notes*) . .	. 1 0	Pro Plancio (*Text and Notes*) .	1 0
In Verrem Actio Prima	. 1 0	Pro Milone	1 0
Pro Lege Manilia, et Pro		Orationes Philippicæ, I., II.	2 0
Archia	. 1 0		

The above, Notes only, in one vol., cloth, 2s. 6d.

De Senectute et De Amicitia 1 0	Epistolæ Selectæ. Pars I.	1 0

CÆSAR.

De Bello Gallico, Lib. i.—iii. (*Text and Notes*) . . . 1 0

CORNELIUS NEPOS.

Vitæ (*Text and Notes*) . . 1 0

PHÆDRUS.

Fabulæ (*Text and Notes*) . 1 0

LIVIUS.

Lib. xxi.—xxiv. (*Text and Notes*) sewed 4 0

Ditto in cloth 4 6

TACITUS.

The Annals. Notes only, 2 vols., 16mo., cloth 7 0

Portions of several other Authors are in preparation.

OCTAVO EDITIONS OF THE CLASSICS.

THE "POETÆ SCENICI GRÆCI," Æschyli, Sophoclis, Euripidis, et Aristophanis, Fabulæ, Superstites, et Perditarum Fragmenta. In recognitione GUIL. DINDORFII. Editio Quinta. Royal 8vo., cloth, 21s.

THUCYDIDES, with Notes, chiefly Historical and Geographical. By the late T. Arnold, D.D. With Indices by the Rev. R. P. C. Tiddeman. Sixth Edition. 3 vols., 8vo., cloth lettered, £1 16s.

THE "TEXT" OF ARNOLD'S THUCYDIDES. The Indices adapted to his Sections, and the Greek Index greatly enlarged, by Tiddeman. 8vo., cloth, 17s.

OXFORD, AND 377, STRAND, LONDON.

OCTAVO EDITIONS OF THE CLASSICS (*continued*).

ÆSCHYLUS.—Æschyli Eumenides ad Codicum Manuscriptorum Fidem recognovit et Notis Manu'am Partem Criticis Instruxit GULIELMUS LINWOOD, M.A., Ædis Christi Alumnus et Reg. Societ. Asiat. Soc, 8vo., cloth, 5s.

ARISTOPHANES.—Aves, edited by BLAYDES. 8vo., 1s.

ARISTOTLE.—Ethics; with English Notes, by WILLIAM EDWARD JELF, H.D., late Student of Christ Church, Oxford. 8vo., cloth, 12s.

ARISTOTLE.—The Rhetoric of Aristotle, with Notes, and illustrated by Parallel Passages from other Works. By the Rev. FREDERIC JAMES PARSONS, B.D., Fellow of Magdalen College, Oxford. 8vo., cloth, 7s.

HERODOTUS.—Tabulæ Herodoti. 8vo., 2s. 6d.

LIVY.—The History of Rome, by Titus Livius. With English Notes. By C. W. STOCKER. 4 vols. 8vo., cloth, 10s.

SOPHOCLES.—The Plays of Sophocles, with Notes Critical and Explanatory, adapted to the use of Schools and Universities, by T. MITCHELL, A.M., late Fellow of Sidney Sussex College, Cambridge. Ajax, Electra, Œdipus Coloneus, Philoctetes, Trachiniæ, 8vo., cloth, 5s. each.

SOPHOCLES.—Sophoclis Œdipus Tyrannus ex Recensione PETRI ELMSLEY, A.M., qui et Annotationes suas adjecit. 8vo., cloth, 2s. 6d.

THUCYDIDES.—Tabulæ Thucydidæ, ex Gailio. 8vo., 2s. 6d.

Translations of the Classics.

ÆSCHYLUS.—Prometheus Chained. Translated by C. C. CLIFFORD, D.C.L. 8vo., 2s.

ARISTOPHANES.—The Frogs of Aristophanes. Translated by C. C. CLIFFORD, D.C.L., Fellow of All Souls' College, Oxford. 8vo., 2s. 6d.

EURIPIDES.—The Bacchæ of Euripides, translated into English Verse; with a Preface, by JAMES E. THOROLD ROGERS. Cr. 8vo., cl., 3s.

HOMER.—A nearly literal Translation of Homer's Odyssey into Accentuated Dramatic Verse. By the Rev. LOVELACE BIGGE-WITHER, M.A. Large fcap. 8vo., toned paper, cloth, 10s. 6d.

SOPHOCLES.—Œdipus, King of Thebes. Translated from the Œdipus Tyrannus of Sophocles by Sir FRANCIS HASTINGS DOYLE, late Fellow of All Souls College, Oxford. 24mo., sewed, 1s.

THUCYDIDES.—The History of the Peloponnesian War by Thucydides, in Eight Books. Book I. Done into English by RICHARD CRAWLEY, of University College, Oxford. 8vo., cloth, 5s.

VIRGIL.—The Georgics of Virgil, literally and rhythmically Translated by WILLIAM SEWELL, B.D., Warden of St. Peter's College, Radley. For the Use of Students. Fcap. 8vo., cloth, 2s. 6d.

English Classics.

THE LIVES OF THE MOST EMINENT ENGLISH POETS; with Critical Observations on their Works. By SAMUEL JOHNSON. 3 vols. 24mo., cloth; 2s. 6d. each. (*Uniform with the Oxford Pocket Classics.*)

OXFORD, AND 377, STRAND, LONDON.

EDUCATIONAL WORKS.

Greek.

JELF'S GREEK GRAMMAR.—A Grammar of the Greek Language, chiefly from the text of Raphael Kühner. By Wm. Edw. Jelf, B.D., late Student and Censor of Ch. Ch. *Fourth Edition; with Additions and Corrections.* 3 vols. 8vo., 1l. 10s.

RUDIMENTARY RULES, with Examples, for the Use of Beginners in Greek Prose Composition. By John Mitchinson, D.C.L., (now Bishop of Barbados). 16mo., sewed, 1s. (*Uniform with Oxford Pocket Classics.*)

LAWS OF THE GREEK ACCENTS. By John Griffiths, D.D., Warden of Wadham College, Oxford. 16mo., price 6d.

Η ΚΑΙΝΗ ΔΙΑΘΗΚΗ. The Greek Testament with English Notes. By the Rev. Edward Burton, D.D., sometime Regius Professor of Divinity in the University of Oxford. Sixth Edition, with index. 8vo., cloth, 10s. 6d.

Latin.

MADVIG'S LATIN GRAMMAR. A Latin Grammar for the Use of Schools. By Professor Madvig, with additions by the Author. Translated by the Rev. G. Woods, M.A. *New Edition, with an Index of Authors.* 8vo., cloth, 12s.

TWELVE RUDIMENTARY RULES FOR LATIN PROSE COM-POSITION; with Examples and Exercises, for the use of Beginners. By the Rev. Edward Moore, D.D., Principal of St. Edmund Hall, Oxford. 16mo., 6d.

ERASMI COLLOQUIA SELECTA; Arranged for Translation and Re-translation; adapted for the Use of Boys who have begun the Latin Syntax. By Edward C. Lowe, D.D. Fcap. 8vo., strong binding, 3s.

POETA LATINA; A Selection from Latin Authors, for Translation and Re-Translation; arranged in a Progressive Course, as an Introduction to the Latin Tongue. By Edward C. Lowe, D.D., Fcap. 8vo., strongly bound, 3s.

SPECIMENS OF COMPOSITION IN PROSE AND VERSE, Latin, French, and English. By Charles Neave, M.A., Fellow of Oriel College, Oxford. Crown 8vo., limp cloth, 3s. 6d.

GULIELMI SHAKESPERII JULIUS CÆSAR. Latine Reddidit Henricus Denison, Coll. Oen. An. apud Oxon. Olim Socius. 8vo., cloth, 6s.

SYLLABUS OF LATIN PRONUNCIATION, drawn up at the request of Head Masters of Schools. 8vo., 3d.

French.

CHOICE EXTRACTS FROM MODERN FRENCH AUTHORS, for the use of Schools. 18mo., cloth, 3s.

SUPPLÉANT DE LA PRATIQUE DU LANGAGE FAMILIER OU APPLICATION DES IDIOTISMES FRANÇAIS. Par Jules Bué, Teacher of French to the University of Oxford. No. 1. La Camaraderie, par Eugène Scribe. 8vo., 4s.

Hebrew.

A GRAMMATICAL ANALYSIS OF THE HEBREW PSALTER; being an Explanatory Interpretation of Every Word contained in the Book of Psalms, intended chiefly for the Use of Beginners in the Study of Hebrew. By Joshua Julia Greenwell. Post 8vo., cloth, 6s.

ANALECTA HEBRAICA; with Critical Notes, and Tables and Paradigms of the Conjugations. By C. W. H. Pauli. With a Key. 8vo., cl., 5s.

AN INTRODUCTION TO HEBREW GRAMMAR, by W. T. Phillips. Second Edition. 8vo., cloth, 12s.

EDUCATIONAL WORKS (continued).

Mathematics.

TREATISE ON TRILINEAR CO-ORDINATES, intended chiefly for the Use of Junior Students. By C. J. C. Price, M.A., Fellow and Lecturer of Exeter College, Oxford. Post 8vo., cloth, 8s.

NOTES ON THE GEOMETRY OF THE PLANE TRIANGLE. By John Griffiths, M.A., Mathematical Lecturer of Jesus College, Oxford. Crown 8vo., cloth, 4s.

THE PROPOSITIONS OF THE FIFTH BOOK OF EUCLID PROVED ALGEBRAICALLY: with an Introduction, Notes, and Questions. By George Stanton Ward, M.A., Mathematical Lecturer in Wadham College and Magdalen Hall, Oxford. Crown 8vo., cloth, 2s. 6d.

A SYLLABUS OF PLANE ALGEBRAICAL GEOMETRY. Systematically arranged, with Formal Definitions, Postulates, and Axioms. By Charles Lutwidge Dodgson, M.A., Student and Mathematical Lecturer of Christ Church, Oxford. 8vo., cloth, 6s.

THE FORMULÆ OF PLANE TRIGONOMETRY, printed with Symbols (instead of Words) to express the "Goniometrical Ratios." By C. L. Dodgson, M.A. 4to., 1s.

THE ENUNCIATIONS OF EUCLID I. TO VI., with Axioms, &c. Fcap. 8vo., 9d.

THE FIFTH BOOK OF EUCLID TREATED ALGEBRAICALLY. By C. L. Dodgson. 8vo., 1s. 6d.

THE THREE FIRST SECTIONS, AND PART OF THE SEVENTH SECTION, OF NEWTON'S PRINCIPIA. With a Preface and an Introduction by George Leigh Cooke, B.D., Sedleian Reader in Natural Philosophy in the University of Oxford. 8vo., cloth, 6s.

Arithmetic.

CLASS BOOK OF ARITHMETIC. By the Rev. D. Edwards, M.A., Mathematical Lecturer at St. John's School, Harstpierpoint. 18mo., 1s.
———————————— with Answers. Cloth, 1s. 6d.

Logic.

ARTIS LOGICÆ RUDIMENTA. Accessit Solutio Sophismatum. In Usum Juventutis Academicæ. 12mo., sewed, 2s. 6d.
———————————— with Illustrative Observations on each Section. By John Hill, B.D., Vice-Principal of St. Edmund Hall, Oxford. Sixth Edition. 12mo., cloth, 3s.

Mechanical Philosophy.

TEXT-BOOK OF MECHANICAL PHILOSOPHY, for the Use of Students. By the Rev. Robert Walker, M.A., F.R.S.; Mathematical Lecturer of Wadham College, and Reader in Experimental Philosophy, Oxford. Part I., Mechanics. Fcap. 8vo., cloth, 5s.
———————————— Part II., Hydrostatics and Pneumatics. Fcap. 8vo., sewed, 2s. 6d.

EDUCATIONAL WORKS (*continued*).

Examination Papers.

EXAMINATION PAPERS IN THE FIRST PUBLIC, *in Literis Graecis et Latinis*, from 1863 to 1871. Printed directly from the Examiners' Copies in the Oxford University Examinations. Selection of 12 Papers. Cloth, 7s. 6d.

———————————— SECOND PUBLIC, *in Literis Humanioribus*, from 1868 to 1873. Selection of 10 Papers. Cloth, 7s. 6d.

———————————— FIRST PUBLIC, *in Disciplinis Mathematicis*. From 1863 to 1873. Selection of 12 Papers. Cloth, 7s. 6d.

———————————— SECOND PUBLIC, *in Scientiis Mathematicis et Physicis*. From 1863 to 1873. Selection of 12 Papers. Cloth, 7s. 6d.

———————————— IN THE SCHOOL OF NATURAL SCIENCE. From 1865 to 1868. Complete, cloth, 7s. 6d.
——————— From 1868 to 1871. Complete, 10 Papers, cloth, 8s.

———————————— IN THE SCHOOL OF THEOLOGY. From 1870 to 1873. Complete, 6 Papers, cloth, 4s.

———————————— IN THE SCHOOL OF LAW AND MODERN HISTORY. From 1867 to 1872. Complete in One Volume, cloth, 7s. 6d.

Many of the Examination Papers contained in the above volumes may be had separately at 1s. each. Also many of the Papers for Responsions between the years 1863 and 1873, price 6d. each.

UNIVERSITY OF OXFORD LOCAL EXAMINATIONS. Examination Papers and Division Lists for the years 1860 and 1861, 8vo., each 3s. 6d.

——————— Examination Papers for the years 1870, 1871, 1872, 1873, each 3s.

——————— Division Lists for the years 1867, 1868, each 1s. 6d.; for the years 1869, 1870, 1871, 1872, 1873, each 2s.

EXAMINATION PAPERS, consisting of Passages selected from Greek and Latin Authors, Prose and Verse; with Questions on the Subject Matter. Edited by J. R. Major, D.D., Head Master of King's College School, London. Specimen Packets, containing 10 Papers, price 1s. Packets of separate Pieces, 24 in number, 1s.

The University of Oxford.

THE OXFORD UNIVERSITY CALENDAR for 1874. Corrected to the end of December, 1873. 12mo., cloth, 4s. 6d.

THE OXFORD TEN-YEAR BOOK: A Complete Register of University Honours and Distinctions, made up to the end of the Year 1870. Crown 8vo., roan, 7s. 6d.

PASS AND CLASS: An Oxford Guide-Book through the Courses of *Literae Humaniores*, Mathematics, Natural Science, and Law and Modern History. By Montagu Burrows, Chichele Professor of Modern History. Third Edition. Revised and Enlarged; with Appendices. Fcap. 8vo., cloth, 5s.

COLLEGIATE and PROFESSORIAL TEACHING and DISCIPLINE, in answer to Professor Vaughan. By the Rev. E. B. Pusey, D.D., Regius Professor of Hebrew. 8vo., cloth, 5s.

THE RE-ORGANIZATION of the UNIVERSITY of OXFORD. By Goldwin Smith. Post 8vo., cloth, 5s.

SCIENTIFIC.

THE ELEMENTS OF PSYCHOLOGY, ON THE PRINCIPLES
OF BENEKE, Stated and Illustrated in a Simple and Popular Manner by
Dr. G. Raue, Professor in the Medical College, Philadelphia; Fourth Edition, considerably Altered, Improved, and Enlarged, by Johann Gottlieb
Dressler, late Director of the Normal School at Bautzen. Translated
from the German. Post 8vo., cloth, 6s.

MISCELLANIES: BEING A COLLECTION OF MEMOIRS
and ESSAYS ON SCIENTIFIC AND LITERARY SUBJECTS, published at Various Times, by the late Charles Daubeny, M.D., F.R.S.,
Professor of Botany in the University of Oxford, &c. 2 vols., 8vo., cloth, 21s.

LECTURES ON ROMAN HUSBANDRY, delivered before the
University of Oxford. By the late Charles Daubeny, M.D., F.R.S., &c.
8vo., cloth, 6s.

ESSAY ON THE TREES and SHRUBS OF THE ANCIENTS:
being the Substance of Four Lectures delivered before the University of
Oxford, intended to be Supplementary to those on Roman Husbandry. By
the late Charles Daubeny, M.D., F.R.S., &c. 8vo., cloth, 3s.

RESULTS OF ASTRONOMICAL AND METEOROLOGICAL
OBSERVATIONS, made at the Radcliffe Observatory, Oxford, in the years
1840 to 1870, under the superintendence of Manuel J. Johnson, M.A., and
the Rev. Robert Main, M.A., Radcliffe Observers. Volumes I. to XXX.
Royal 8vo., cloth, each 15s.

THE RADCLIFFE CATALOGUE OF 6,317 STARS, chiefly
Circumpolar, reduced to the Epoch 1845.0; formed from the Observations
made at the Radcliffe Observatory, Oxford, under the Superintendence of
Manuel John Johnson, M.A., with an Introduction by the Rev. Robert
Main, M.A. Royal 8vo., cloth, £1 1s.

SECOND RADCLIFFE CATALOGUE, containing 2,386 STARS;
deduced from Observations extending from 1854 to 1861, at the Radcliffe
Observatory, Oxford; and reduced to the Epoch 1860, under the superintendence of the Rev. Robert Main, M.A. Royal 8vo., cloth, 15s.

ATOMIC WEIGHTS, by A. H. Church. On card, 8d.; paper, 2d.

LABELS for REAGENTS, by A. H. Church. On large sheet, 6d.

THE PRINCIPLES OF CURRENCY: Six Lectures delivered at
Oxford. By Bonamy Price, Professor of Political Economy in the University of Oxford. With a Letter from M. Michel Chevalier, on the
History of the Treaty of Commerce with France. 8vo., cloth, 7s. 6d.

MEMOIR on the CHOLERA AT OXFORD in the YEAR 1854,
with Considerations Suggested by the Epidemic. By Henry Wentworth
Acland, M.D., &c., Regius Professor of Medicine in the University of
Oxford. 4to., cloth, 12s.

SYNOPSIS OF THE PHYSIOLOGICAL SERIES IN THE
CHRIST CHURCH MUSEUM, Arranged for the Use of Students. By
Henry W. Acland, M.B., &c. 4to., cloth, 2s. 6d.

HISTORICAL WORKS.

English History.

THE NEW SCHOOL-HISTORY OF ENGLAND, from Early
Writers and the National Records. By the Author of "The Annals of England."
Fifth Thousand. Crown 8vo, with Four Maps, limp cloth, 5s.

OPINIONS OF THE PRESS.

"School-histories are generally mere abridgments of some larger work, or at best compilations from several rather than the results of original investigation. This may fairly be styled a new one, from its being constructed on the new plan of consulting original authorities, and thus showing how light on events and persons hitherto misrepresented and misunderstood. Not satisfied with traditional views, the writer has examined the earliest writers, the State-in-book, the Public Records, and the various works lately issued by authority, and carefully weighed all the evidence within reach. The result is a far more accurate account of our history than can be found in ordinary text-books."—*Athenæum.*

"We are glad to draw attention to 'The New School-History of England,' by the author of 'The Annals of England.' English history has been enriched of late from so many new sources, and illustrated by so many able commentators that—while the

older style of text-books, such as Goldsmith and his followers, have become completely obsolete—even the more recent compilations of Dr. smith, founded as they are upon these, have ceased to represent the actual state of knowledge. This appears to be done so well and the spirit will allow in this book before us. Facts there are not, so that need to be, wisely divided; and the social and political characteristics of the different periods are clearly marked."—*Guardian.*

"Here is a book of no ordinary value; and, as the author justly says, it differs most advantageously from most English Histories for Schools. ... The necessary condensation, which would prevent the great difficulty in carrying out the scheme given above, has been very well accomplished, and our readers may with perfect confidence order this book for the use of their children, while many might with advantage read their own historical studies under its humble but judicious guidance."—*John Bull.*

THE ANNALS OF ENGLAND. An Epitome of English History.
From Cotemporary Writers, the Rolls of Parliament, and other Public Records.
3 vols. Fcap. 8vo, with Illustrations, cloth, 15s.
Vol. I. From the Roman Era to the Death of Richard II. Cloth, 5s.
Vol. II. From the Accession of the House of Lancaster to Charles I. Cloth, 5s.
Vol. III. From the Commonwealth to the Death of Queen Anne. Cloth, 5s.

—— A LIBRARY EDITION, revised and enlarged, with additional
Woodcuts. 8vo. *[Nearly ready.*

A CONTINUATION of the above, from the Accession of George I. to the
Present Time. *[In preparation.*

Historical, &c.

LECTURES ON THE STUDY OF HISTORY, DELIVERED IN
OXFORD, 1859—61. By GOLDWIN SMITH, late Regius Professor of Modern
History in the University of Oxford. *Second Edition.* Crown 8vo, limp cl., 3s. 6d.

IRISH HISTORY AND IRISH CHARACTER. By GOLDWIN
SMITH. *Second Edition.* Post 8vo, 5s.

—— Cheap Edition, Fcap. 8vo, sewed, 1s. 6d.

ARYAN CIVILIZATION, its Religious Origin and its Progress, with
an Account of the Religion, Laws, and Institutions of Greece and Rome, based
on the work of DE COULANGES. By the Rev. T. CHILDE BARKER, Vicar of
Uptalsbury, Oxfordshire, and late Student of Christ Church. Crown 8vo, cl., 5s.

ARE WE BETTER THAN OUR FATHERS? or, A Comparative
View of the Social Position of England at the Revolution of 1688, and at the
Present Time. FOUR LECTURES delivered in St. Paul's Cathedral in
November, 1871. By ROBERT GREGORY, M.A., Canon of St. Paul's. Crown
8vo, 2s. 6d.

A CHART OF ANCIENT HISTORY, by P. H. C. SMITH. Mounted
on roller, price 10s. 6d.

OXFORD, AND 377, STRAND, LONDON.

MISCELLANEOUS.

DE POETICÆ VI MEDICA. Prælectiones Academicæ Oxonii Habitæ, Annis MDCCCXXII.—MDCCCXLI., a Joanne Keble, A.M., Poëticæ Publico Prælectore, Collegii Oriclensis Nuper Soc'o. 2 vols., 8vo., cl., 10s. 6d.

PRÆLECTIONES ACADEMICÆ IN HOMERUM, Oxonii Habitæ, Ann's MDCCLXXVI.—MDCCLXXXIII., a JOANNE RANDOLPH, S.T.P., Poëticæ Publico Prælectore, Postea Episcopo Londinensi. 8vo., cloth, 7s. 6d.

AN ESSAY ON THE ANCIENT WEIGHTS AND MONEY, AND THE ROMAN AND GREEK LIQUID MEASURES, &c. By the Rev. ROBERT MCCASBY, M.A., Student of Christ Church. 8vo., cloth, 7s. 6d.

THE EMPIRE. A SERIES OF LETTERS PUBLISHED IN "THE DAILY NEWS," 1862, 1863. By GOLDWIN SMITH. Post 8vo., cloth, price 6s.

NORWAY: The Road and the Fell. By CHARLES ELTON, late Fellow of Queen's College, Oxford. Post 8vo., cloth, 7s. 6d.

TEN MONTHS IN THE FIJI ISLANDS. By Mrs. SMYTHE. With Introduction, &c., by Maj.-Gen. W. J. SMYTHE, Royal Artillery, late H.M. Commissioner to Fiji. Maps and coloured Plates. 8vo., cloth, 10s.

FUGITIVE POEMS, relating to Subjects connected with Natural History and Physical Science, Archæology, &c. Selected by the late CHARLES DAUBENY, &c. Fcap. 8vo., cloth, 5s.

LAYS OF THE ENGLISH CAVALIERS. By JOHN J. DANIELL, Perpetual Curate of Langley Fitzurse, Wilts. Small 4to., printed on toned paper, with Frontispiece and Vignette, ornamental cloth extra, gilt edges, 6s.

A FRAGMENT OF THE IASON LEGEND. By HENRY HAYMAN, D.D., Head Master of Rugby School. Fcap. 8vo., cloth, 5s.

FASCICULUS. Ediderunt LUDOVICUS GIDLEY et ROBINSON THORN-TON. Fcap. 8vo., cloth, 6s.

EPITAPHS FOR COUNTRY CHURCHYARDS. Collected and Arranged by AUGUSTA. J. C. HARE, of University College, Oxford. Fcap. 8vo., cloth, 2s. 6d.

In the Press.

A LIFE OF BISHOP HERBERT, in which his Letters are incorporated. By EDWARD MEYRICK GOULBURN, D.D., Dean of Norwich, and HENRY SYMONDS, M.A., Precentor of Norwich Cathedral.

Also, THE SERMONS OF HERBERT LOSINGA, first Bishop of Norwich (A.D. 1080—1119), now first edited from a MS. in the Library of the University of Cambridge, with an English Translation and English Notes. 2 vols., 8vo.

www.ingramcontent.com/pod-product-compliance
Lightning Source LLC
Chambersburg PA
CBHW021536270326
41930CB00008B/1272